My sweet
PARIS

CAROLINE MIGNOT
PHOTOGRAPHS **PIERRE-OLIVIER SIGNE**
INTERIOR ILLUSTRATIONS **YANN LE BRAS**
COVER ILLUSTRATION **MARINA VANDEL**

CHÊNE

Foreword

*D*o all great pastries come from Paris? It's entirely possible. The Saint-Honoré is said to have been created in 1847 by Chiboust on rue Saint-Honoré, the religieuse in 1856 at the Frascati pastry shop on rue de Richelieu, the mille-feuille in 1867 at Seugnot's on rue du Bac, and the Paris-Brest in 1891 in a Paris suburb. After years of classicism, monotonous chocolates and ice creams, sleepy tea salons and the usual Sunday pastries, sweets have taken on new life. The city is bubbling over with tastes, sensations, and the inventiveness of artisans buoyed by their success, always looking for new ways to stand out from the crowd. Among them are maestros who know how to transform the most basic ingredients into transcendent delicacies, but also young chefs, trained in Paris or abroad, creating daring fusions of exotic flavors presented in interesting, original spaces.

Paris is filled with infinite ways to satisfy your sweet tooth. I am a food journalist with a lifelong love of desserts, and I had a dream: to criss-cross Paris in search of its sugary treasures and describe them in such delectable detail that heads would swoon, mouths would water in anticipation, and eyes would sparkle with the gluttonous desire to taste each one. I covered the city in search of the sweet and the sublime and came up with this collection of my most delicious finds. As you turn each page, I hope you'll enjoy reading about each of my tastings and sneak out at your first opportunity to get yourself a treat.

Gontran Cherrier

L'Atelier des Chefs

Berthillon

Stéphane Vandermeersch

Shangri-La

Prince de Galles

CAFÉ POUCHKINE

Café Pouchkine

Dominique Saibron

Contents

★ The Classics — 07

★ New Creations — 27

★ Baked Desserts — 41

★ Chocolate — 53

★ Confectionery — 79

★ Frozen Desserts — 87

★ Where to Eat — 97

★ Where to Learn — 115

★ Addresses (in alphabetical order) — 121

★ Addresses (by location) — 130

The Classics

A mille-feuille falling apart as my fork breaks through
the top layer, devouring cream puffs in a corner while
watching a bride and groom on the dance floor, finishing
off an after-school éclair in three gluttonous bites:
I'll never forget the classic French desserts that forged my
love of pastries. Fallen out of fashion for a time or poorly
reproduced in factories, classic pastries have now made
a comeback in the hands of chefs who understand what
makes them so delectable: flavor and freshness.
A crispy puff pastry with the taste of real butter, refreshing
whipped cream, glossy, flavorful icing — the difference is
in the details!

Polonaise
La Pâtisserie des Martyrs

A brioche pastry crust topped with delicate vanilla cream and golden rum-soaked raisins, covered in a thin, crisp layer of meringue: the miniature version (like all of the pastries here) will have you hooked! The Mussipontain is another must: almond meringue, vanilla cream, and crunchy bits of roasted almond. And don't forget their fruit tarts, like the apple tart (tarte aux pommes), whose multiple thin layers resemble those of a mille-feuille, and the extremely refreshing orange tart (tarte aux suprêmes d'orange fraîche), with chunks of fresh orange.

La Pâtisserie des Martyrs? Known to Parisians from the Delicabar, Sébastien Gaudard opened his first shop with the idea of focusing only on the classics, from the most famous traditional desserts to old recipes dug out of vintage cookbooks that are a pleasure to (re)discover. The shop's early 20th century decor catches the eye of many a passerby. (See also pages 46 and 80.)

Vanilla Mille-feuille
Carl Marletti

You cut in with your fork and knife and everything collapses. No worries! This is perfectly normal. It's what makes a mille-feuille such fun to eat! Pile as much as you can onto your fork and bring it up to your mouth. The rich vanilla cream seems to be the perfect companion for the layers of puff pastry. Lightly caramelized, the puff pastry maintains its crunch and might seem overcooked to some (I should warn you, it's almost brown in color), but this is exactly what yields its flavors and sensations. The lemon tart (tarte au citron) is another worthy item here (the lemon cream has a nice degree of tartness and the pâte sablée crust, much like that of a Breton sablé cookie, is perfect.)

Carl Marletti? At the bottom of the rue Mouffetard, in the 5th arrondissement, the discreet shop of this pastry chef is a fixture, offering traditional pastries as well as bold new creations (though, personally, I prefer his interpretations of the classics.)

♥ Saint-Dominique
Gâteaux Thoumieux

This light brioche draws its inspiration from the sugar tart. Before being baked the dough is hollowed out in several places and heavy, double cream poured into the holes then, sprinkled with a little dark brown sugar. It had dried somewhat when I tasted it, which gave a delicious sweet and sour sensation... First, one piece then, a second, it was so easy to eat that it was difficult to stop. The simple, easy to transport 'travel' cakes re-created from chef Jean-François Piège's life experiences and childhood memories are a beautiful tribute to regional France (Saint-Genix pralines, Corsican clementines, Toulouse violets); the seasonal fruit tarts are a delight of simplicity and indulgence.

Gâteaux Thoumieux? This is the recently opened patisserie of famed chef, Jean-François Piège, which just happens to be across the road from his two restaurants. Pastry chef Ludovic Chaussards' cakes are elegantly and desirably displayed in a minimalist setting designed by India Madhavi.

For addresses, see page 121.

1. Pastry chef Sébastien Gaudard
   of La Pâtisserie des Martyrs
2. Pastries at La Pâtisserie des Martyrs
3. Pastry chef Carl Marletti
4. The Saint Dominique at Gâteaux Thoumieux
5. Inside the Gâteau Thoumieux patisserie

1. Gérard Mulot's *fraisier*
2. Gérard Mulot's Amaryllis
3. The display case at Gérard Mulot
4. The chocolate tart at La Petite Rose
5. Showcase at Liberté's
6. The Cream Tart by Benoît Castel,
   Liberté's baker and pastry chef

Cream Tart
Liberté, Boulangerie-Pâtisserie by Benoît Castel

A Mount Everest of Chantilly delicately perfumed with vanilla and a little sugar, hides a pastry cream heart nestled in a thin, crunchy crust—one bite will gently transport you to the heights of pleasure. Not only that, these days, cream tarts are extremely rare in patisseries! The bobo au rhum served in a verrine, bathed in rum syrup and dressed with cream, proudly joins the prestigious baba category because it is so good (and even comes with its own pipette of rum… in case you need a touch more). And, finally, don't miss the bakery section with its array of croissants and *pains au chocolat*, large pieces of take-away brioche, generous chocolate flecked madeleines and divine *fars Bretons* (traditional Brittany flans).

Liberté? The lab-type kitchen opens into the shop—a meeting of two worlds—industrial neon lights and a sleek marble counter. The space was designed by its pastry chef Benoît Castel, formerly with the Bon Marche's La Grande Épicerie, who wanted to create something other than a classic setting. As for the products, they are simple yet very appealing and just within reach on the counter top, tempting you to take all of them…

Seasonal Fruit
I won't say how many shops carry apricot tarts and fraisiers all year long (using frozen or canned fruit), but it has to stop! I urge you to choose fruit pastries only when the fruit is in peak season. I assure you, you will not be disappointed.

Fraisier
Gérard Mulot

A soft genoise biscuit, an almost mousse-like cream lightly flavored with vanilla, and last but not least, strawberries picked at the height of their flavor: this is a thoroughly authentic fraisier. Fruit is indeed the new hot item in this shop. I highly recommend trying the sublime Cacia entremets (blackcurrant-flavored mousse, crispy rice cracker, and green apple with cinnamon) or the extraordinary Blueberry.

Gérard Mulot? The success of his bakery-catering-pastry shop, which opened in Paris forty years ago, is obvious from the moment you set foot inside: there is always a huge crowd. You have to make your choice quickly and the enormous selection of desserts does not make it easy. (See also page 42.)

Chocolate Tart
La Petite Rose

Near perfection. With a lightly cocoa-flavored pâte sablée crust, bits of nougatine and cocoa peppering a refreshing ganache (yes, sometimes a very chocolatey ganache can produce a sensation of freshness in the mouth), and a strong chocolate flavor, this dessert is made for chocolate tart lovers. Also not to be missed, the Marius, a chocolate-chestnut entremets on a puff pastry base with a touch of rum. And don't forget the chocolate bonbons!

La Petite Rose? Miyuki Watanabe is a Japanese-born pastry chef who studied in France before opening her own shop. The day I visited, my mouth was watering at the sight of all her chocolate desserts.

For addresses, see page 121.

Chocolate Tart
Didier Fourreau

Simple in appearance, it brings together two indispensable elements: an ultra-fine (and very buttery) sablé crust and a ganache that is high in cocoa and not overly sweet. I should add that the texture of the ganache is wonderfully silky, which elevates this tart into the pantheon of greats! Note: desserts are sold only on Friday and Saturday.

Didier Fourreau? This talented artisan took over the old Charpentier chocolate shop after ten years in its loyal service. The range of desserts offers a beautiful selection of chocolate bonbons and bars, as well as chocolate desserts at the end of the week.

Praline Éclair
L'Éclair de Génie

One layer of choux pastry on the bottom, another on the top, and between the two (like a Paris-Brest), an airy praline-flavored cream, a thin layer of pure crunchy praline, and some toasted almonds — delicious! Passion fruit-raspberry, vanilla-pecan, and other flavors are available. There is one drawback, though: while all of the éclairs are beautiful and enticing, they're so darn small (and at the same price as, or higher than, éclairs sold elsewhere)! Three bites and you're done.

L'Éclair de Génie? This shop devoted to the éclair (and to chocolate truffles, which I'm less fond of) is the brainchild of Christophe Adam, who had already breathed life back into the éclair as creative director at Fauchon (where he invented the memorable 'La Joconde' or 'Mona Lisa' éclair).

♥ Caramel Éclair
Cyril Lignac

With this rendition, I suddenly understand the meaning of the word 'éclair' — it's gone in a flash. The very thin choux pastry seems to be mostly a pretext, leaving the spotlight to the salty caramel cream. I should warn you, the baba au rhum, soaked and topped with sugarless vanilla whipped cream, is also irresistible. And the raspberry tart (tarte aux framboises) — I have never seen one so gorgeous! The perfectly textured sablé crust rests under a flavorful almond cream, a light vanilla cream, and a perfect line of incredibly aromatic raspberries. It's a real work of art, shining with the brilliant juice that bursts out of each raspberry — truly a masterpiece!

La Pâtisserie by Cyril Lignac? The owner of three restaurants in Paris, this heavily publicized chef teamed up with pastry chef Benoît Couvrand, formerly of Fauchon, to open a pastry shop-bakery. The classics are simply presented, but — careful! — almost addictive. (See also page 46.)

For addresses, see page 121.

1. A box of éclairs at L'Éclair de Génie
2. Passion fruit-raspberry éclairs at
   L'Éclair de Génie
3. The display case at La Pâtisserie
   by Cyril Lignac
4. The Equinoxe at La Pâtisserie by Cyril Lignac

1. A box of Popelini's cream puffs
2. The display case at Popelini
3. Pastry chef Mori Yoshida
4. The Mont-Blanc and the M at Mori Yoshida
5. Other pastries at Mori Yoshida

Chou
Popelini

So round and adorable, these glazed cream puffs look like little jewels that one just has to have (and taste) right away. The dough is soft and fresh, the cream generous, and the sticky icing laid on thick in a way that I happen to like. For a snack or dessert (two appropriate moments), the portion is three cream puffs per person, which seems about right to me: I choose milk chocolate-passion fruit, praline, and the 'chou of the day' filled with whipped cream and bits of caramel.

Popelini? It's the name of the Italian pastry chef who is said to have invented cream puff dough in 1540. Lauren Koumetz, founder of this single-product shop, surrounds herself with fine pastry chefs who prepare each day's batch of cream puffs and help to create new recipes for every season.

Mori Yoshida

While the M might not strictly be considered a classic, Mori Yoshida's other pastries are, so I prefer to include him in this chapter. The M is a three-dimensional triangle of fresh dark chocolate mousse (with precisely the right amount of cocoa and just barely sweetened), an out-of-this-world cream that tastes like something between caramel and maple syrup, a little bitterness from a layer of mandarin jam, and a crunchy biscuit base: it is out of this world! The praline mille-feuille is another delight. Its very dense and rich cream reminds me right away of the buttery cream of a Paris-Brest and its puff pastry layers stay light and crunchy (even into the early evening!).

Mori Yoshida? A Japanese pastry chef who opened his shop in Paris in the spring of 2013, having trained in France and having won a Top Chef-type pastry contest in Japan. Against a backdrop of bare, immaculate cream-colored walls, the desserts seem to float inside the display case. I've never seen anything like it! (See also page 50.)

Macarons

I have a confession to make: I think I've tasted enough macarons to fill three lifetimes. Ten years ago I found them elegant, sublime, and delicious; today I almost can't bear the sight of them. Nonetheless, of all these tasting experiences, I do remember one shop where the macarons were positively grandiose: Pierre Hermé. In my opinion, you have to stick with the simple flavors (blends of more than two are too complex): Infiniment Caramel, Infiniment Vanille, or Mogador (milk chocolate-passion fruit).

For addresses, see page 121.

Raspberry-Rose Saint-Honoré
Ladurée

Pink curls of cream speckled with raspberries and pastry cream-filled choux capped with pink icing, pose on a puff pastry bed. Impressive! In spite of its size, each mouthful of the Saint-Honoré, from beginning to end, was as light as a cloud. Its acidulated notes of raspberry and rose have the gift of creating poetry in the mouth. It brought to mind the Ispahan, invented by Pierre Hermé when he was Ladurée's head pastry chef, and which is still on their menu. Worth discovering too is the Divin, a macaron look-alike with an exquisite harmony of almond, nougat and raspberry flavours. And, don't forget the very gourmet Succès Praliné—an almond biscuit base topped with praline cream and napped with milk chocolate.

Ladurée? It was originally opened as a bakery on rue Royale in 1862 by Louis Ernest Ladurée. Following a fire on the premises in 1871, it was converted to a pastry shop and decorated by Jules Chéret, the famous painter, known for his poster art. Now, the location's aesthetic beauty, as well as its pastries, attracts visitors from around the world.

Tiramisu
Pâtisserie de l'Église

Today, this dessert is so rare in shops that I couldn't resist trying it on my first visit. Served in a half sphere (which looked like chocolate but was actually plastic, reusable for in-house desserts), this tiramisu is just what it should be: a creamy mascarpone mousse base with cafe-imbibed biscuits (my preference), a hint of amaretto to warm the throat and a few thin, chocolate wafers inserted for a bit of crispiness. Also, I really loved their mango-raspberry tart: a crunchy sugar pastry crust filled with an almond cream, covered with whole raspberries and topped with pretty balls of mango mousse and slices of mango confit.

Pâtisserie de l'Église? Opened in 1887, this pastry shop is just across from Belleville's Saint Jean-Baptiste church. The talent of the owners, the Demoncy and Levergne families, has allowed them to combine old world charm with innovation; it is a place where one is always well received.

Perfect Timing

Don't forget to remove pastries from the refrigerator at least 15 minutes before serving. But don't take them out too early, either. After 30 minutes, cream-based desserts will start to warm and will have passed their peak of flavor and texture.

For addresses, see page 121.

1. Ladurée's raspberry-rose Saint-Honoré
2. A dining room in Ladurée Champs-Elysées
3. Inside the Pâtisserie de l'Eglise boutique
4. The Tiramisu at the Pâtisserie de l'Eglise

1. Cornes de gazelle at the Gazelle d'Or bakery
2. Assorted Moroccan pastries at the Gazelle d'Or
3. Inside the Scoop Me a Cookie shop
4. A large cookie from Scoop Me a Cookie
5. Cookies at Scoop Me a Cookie

Corne de gazelle
Gazelle d'Or

The quality of this Moroccan specialty is the delicate pastry, which gently holds everything together during baking. The thin layer of pastry contains an almond filling perfumed with the fragrance of orange blossoms. Bliss! Better take a few of these, as well as the others, because each one only has a couple of deliciously dainty bites... Try the chebbakia, intertwined fried pastry rings flavoured with cinnamon, aniseed and sesame, drenched in honey and with a delicate orange blossom scent—a wonderful marriage of flavours. Then, there's the crumbly, melt-in-the mouth sesame-cinnamon biscuit known as a ghriba which is a taste treat. And, don't overlook the briouats au miel or the cigares aux amandes.

Gazelle d'or? Hassan Ichouan is the creator behind this brand name. His shop's window is one of a traditional bakery which certainly hides its game—once inside you will discover an incredible collection of cakes giving you the opportunity to discover typically Moroccan pastries.

♥ Je t'épouse dans l'heure
Scoop Me a Cookie

Peanut butter, whole peanuts, pretzels (with salt crystals) and milk chocolate, undulate on the surface of this large, very addictive cookie. Weighing twice as much a classic cookie, every mouthful is eaten with the same joyful anticipation: What am I going to find? A bit of milk chocolate, a peanut, or maybe some pretzel...? The whimsical Kinder heart cookie is a combination of the Oreo cookie's chocolaty taste with morsels of Kinder bar (one of the few industrial chocolate bars I am unable to resist). Just as impressive are the giant cookies (cookie-cakes to share), the whoopies (cream filling sandwiched between two cookies), and the Glouton filled with Kinder cream and coated with salted butter caramel and peanuts.

Scoop Me a Cookie? As soon as you enter, it is impossible to tear your eyes away from the fun and fanciful cookies of Laura Petit. The shop also has a small, pleasant area with a sofa and coffee table where you can linger for a coffee-cookie break.

Speculoos Waffle
Meert

The first time I tasted it, I expected the crust to be crispy (which is silly, it's not a wafer). In reality, the fine dough is soft, offering a light resistance. The crunch — because there is definitely a crunch — is in the filling. The speculoos cream is generously loaded with brown sugar that crackles under your teeth, with a very present speculoos flavor. A northern delight!

Meert? A pastry institution in Lille since 1761, though its name dates back only to 1849, around the time Mr. Meert, of Flemish heritage, started making this flat waffle filled with sugar, butter, and vanilla. With its pastel tones, woodwork, and hatboxes (filled with waffles), the candy-store decor of the Parisian shop, opened in the heart of the Marais in 2010, makes it feel like a fairytale.

 Merveilleux
Fred

Beneath the slightly outdated look of these domes hide infinite layers of soft meringue and light whipped cream that make you feel as if you are biting into a cloud. The chocolate version, with dark chocolate-flavored cream and dark chocolate shavings, and the speculoos flavor, with speculoos-flavored cream and white chocolate shavings, are my two favorites (it also comes in praline, coffee, and cherry). Choose from several sizes: mini, individual, or a large, shareable cake.

Aux Merveilleux de Fred? The pastry chef Frédéric Vaucamps started making this traditional cake in the late 1990s. Since then, his Lille-based shop has multiplied across the north side of Paris, each boutique operating on the same principle: the Merveilleux are prepared continuously throughout the day, under the covetous eyes of customers who can't help but be tempted.

The Memory of Taste

Whether we first discovered them in Saint-Jean-de-Luz, Lille, or Bordeaux, these specialties are often associated with a happy memory — a sunny vacation, an enchanted weekend. Gustatory or taste memories always recall what is good, what makes an instant precious, so don't hesitate to create more of these special moments. Head straight to Pariès, Meert, or Baillardran!

For addresses, see page 121.

1. Meert
2. Meert's waffles
3. Different flavors of Fred's Merveilleux
4. Inside Aux Merveilleux de Fred

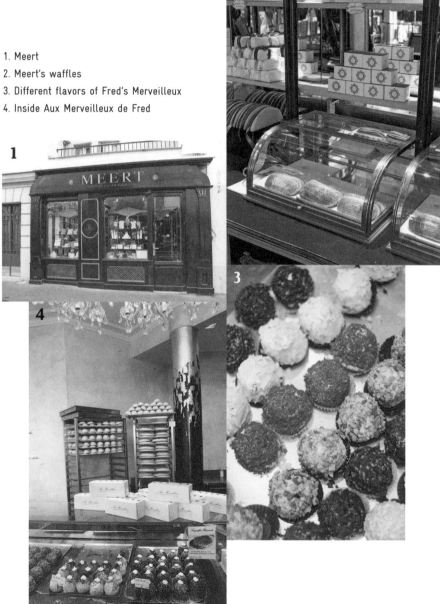

1. A chocolate-nougatine pastry at Pariès
2. Mouchous at Pariès
3. Baillardran's *canelé*
4. Baillardran
5. Le Comptoir Baulois
6. The Fondants Baulois

Mouchou
Pariès

With its two joined shells of biscuit meringué and its spherical shape, the Mouchou looks like it could be an ancestor of the modern, sophisticated macaron. Except that the flavors of Mouchou offered at Pariès are those of simple yet very flavorful nuts. With their palpable generosity, their salient flavors of almond, toasted pine nuts, intense pistachio, or a hazelnut that is almost a praline, these big Mouchous, dare I say, almost make me feel better about macarons.

Pariès? This hundred-year-old shop in Saint-Jean-de-Luz manipulates sugar, almonds, and chocolate with an ever-present concern for quality. All of the traditional Basque desserts are magnificently represented: chocolate, touron, gâteau Basque, etc. You can leave with a sample of each! (See also page 83.)

Canelé
Baillardran

With a nicely browned and slightly sticky crust, it has a sponge-like aspect on the inside which adds a light airiness to the soft dough — and for the better: this rendition perfectly embodies the duality that should exist in a cannelé between the inside and the outside (which is the result of baking for a long time in a hot oven). With a hint of rum and a vanilla flavor that lingers on the palate, it is sure to thrill fans of this Bordeaux specialty. Personally, I like the medium-sized version: it fills your mouth (unlike the small one, which feels like not enough) while leaving room in your belly (unlike the large version) for one or two more.

For addresses, see page 121.

Baillardran? Upon his return from the U.S. in 1987, pastry chef Philippe Baillardran decided to go into the cannelé business, opening a first shop in Bordeaux, followed by several others, notably in Paris.

♥ Fondant Baulois
Comptoir Baulois

This innocent looking cake hides its secret well. Under a very thin crispy exterior, the texture inside is so soft that it's almost creamy. It's a rather surprising contrast. Moreover, the generous chocolate flavor of the cream finishes with a slight note of salted butter caramel. The other specialty of the shop is the gâteau Nantais, a cake lightly infused with rum and covered with sugary icing. Being from Nantes myself, I can tell you: this is the genuine article!

Le Comptoir Baulois? The recipe is kept secret by Marie-Sophie and Stéphane Bouillier at their workshop in La Baule, in the Loire-Atlantique region of France. Their Paris branch is set up in an old bookstore, shelves and all, which makes it a nice place to sit down for a snack.

♥ Pastel de Nata
Comme à Lisbonne

It is the only thing sold at this shop counter, other than the few Portuguese products (coffee, olive oil, etc.) that line a few shelves in the corner. Made of a thin, crisp, flaky crust filled with an egg-based cream (whose richness comes from its high proportion of yolks), the pastel de nata is served warm and dusted with cinnamon, if desired. Exactly as in Lisbon! In the heart of Paris, at 11 a.m., with a short espresso — suddenly, you feel like you are in another country.

Comme à Lisbonne? Victor Silveira has done a marvelous job adapting his mother's recipe for this little cream tartlet, invented in a monastery in the 17th century and made for almost 200 years by the Pastéis de Belém pastry shop in Lisbon.

Carrot Cake
Bread & Roses

Here, this favorite of English and American dessert lovers has everything you want in a carrot cake: a soft, moist cake, slightly tart and refreshing cream cheese, and its characteristic flavor, a blend of carrot, cinnamon, nuts, and sugar. Bread & Roses, which never does things halfway, doubles the layer of cream and decorates the top with rounds of candied carrot — not to mention that it comes in a portion that would satisfy Gulliver himself.

Bread & Roses? Bakery, pastry shop, caterer, and tea salon, this shop is the brainchild of Philippe Tailleur, a Frenchman enamored of England. The bread and pastries are generous in flavor and in size!

♥ Rachel's Cheesecake
Rachel's Cakes

I might as well tell you straight away, this is one of my favorite Anglo-American desserts. I've tried quite a few and Rachel Moeller's is absolutely perfect. A very thin layer of immaculate cream on top (reminiscent of a thick petit-suisse), a slightly different cream beneath, with a hint of tartness, then a crunchy crust at the base, distinguished by a touch of speculoos — it's divine! Start with the plain version if you've never had cheesecake before. Then try the green tea flavor, which will blow you away.

Rachel's Cakes? An American cake shop that began by providing restaurants with the best cheesecake in Paris. [Some try to hide that it's Rachel's they're serving, but if you've tasted it once, you'll recognize it right away.] Happily, Rachel has decided to open her own shop in the Marais in early 2014 (the date had not been confirmed at the time of printing).

For addresses, see page 121.

1. The carrot cake at Bread & Roses
2. Inside Bread & Roses
3. Comme à Lisbonne's *pastéis de nata*
4. The cheesecake at Rachel's Cakes

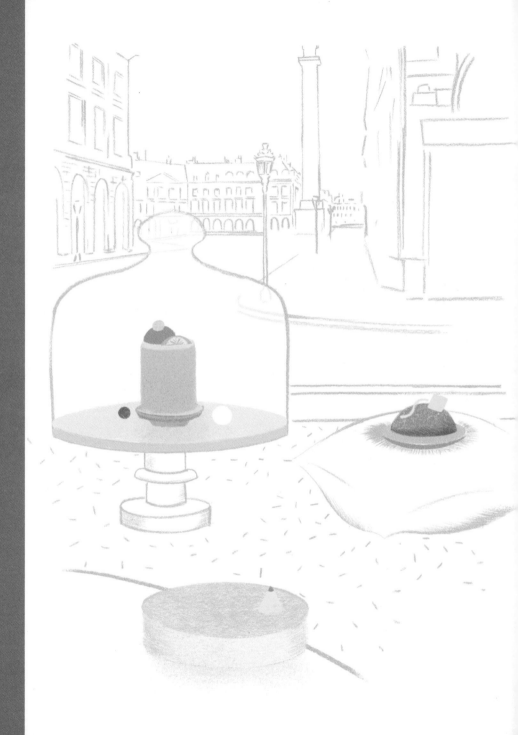

New Creations

It's reassuring to indulge in comforting classics, but it can also be quite intoxicating to succumb to the allure of a new adventure. We expect surprises, emotions, discovery, and delectation from our pastry chefs! Bizarre shapes, strange colors, chocolate that we never dreamed existed, with spices, flowers, aromatic plants, or unusual fruits. When artisans create desserts from scratch, the results can be disastrously gluttonous! Go ahead, give in to temptation.

Ispahan
Pierre Hermé

My first few years in this profession were so filled with his macarons that I had never taken the time to taste his most famous creation, a flavor combination that has inspired many a pastry chef. Through Pierre Hermé's imagination, raspberry, rose, and lychee transform into two macaron shells enclosing fresh raspberries, a rose-flavored cream, and bits of lychee, creating a moment of poetry in your mouth. Poetry? Yes, in the exotic, tart, floral notes that come together to comprise something rather delicate. The Infiniment Vanille tart is another jewel. Pierre Hermé chose to assemble three vanillas of different origins to arrive at his particular conception of the flavor. Piled onto a sablé crust, the vanilla creams sing together in joyful harmony.

Pierre Hermé? Many consider him a god of pastry, since he was the one who first brought pastry back into the spotlight. Macarons with unusual flavor combinations, collaborations with a perfume expert — Pierre Hermé takes risks and always comes out on top. (See also page 65.)

Popucino
La Fabrique à Gâteaux

Although I'm not a fan of coffee-flavored desserts in general (I don't like sweetened coffee) nor of desserts with alcohol, I can honestly say that the Popucino won me over. A chocolate shell filled with a coffee-and-Bailey's-flavored mousse and topped with a light whipped cream, all sitting on a crunchy pecan praline crust — what's not to like? The Wetka, a tart filled with peanuts, gooey caramel, and bits of milk chocolate, is also exquisite. And the milky, tart flavors of the cheesecake with candied morello cherries are very refreshing.

La Fabrique à Gâteaux? A shop opened by Alice Le Baron and Lisa Leclerc, who trained at the Ferrandi School of Culinary Arts, then with the famous pastry chef Gérard Mulot. From the counter, you can see the pretty blue laboratory and smell the irresistible aromas of freshly baked desserts. They also bake large cakes to order. Personally, I am happy to see more talented women working in pastry!

Ispahan

Rose, fresh raspberry, and lychee is a flavor combination created in 1987 by pastry chef Pierre Hermé, who named it after the ancient Persian capital. Many times copied, but never equaled, the Ispahan has now become a benchmark in the world of pastry, on a par with the Saint-Honoré or the Opéra.

For addresses, see page 121.

1. Pierre Hermé's Ispahans
2. Inside one of Pierre Hermé's shops
3. Pastries at La Fabrique à Gâteaux
4. La Fabrique à Gâteaux
5. The Popucino at La Fabrique à Gâteaux

1. The Napoléon at Café Pouchkine
2. Macarons and tarts at Café Pouchkine
3. The display case at Café Pouchkine
4. Inside La Pâtisserie des Rêves

♥ *Calisson*
La Pâtisserie des Rêves

Lightly crispy meringue on top, smooth orange- and orange-blossom-flavored cream, a thin layer of almond paste dotted with candied fruit, and a crunchy praline base: this series of layers forming a kind of entremets is a sublime homage to the confectionery of Aix-en-Provence. Sticking with the 'calisson' theme, the Calisson Sablé is diabolical (a very buttery biscuit, with a fine layer of calisson-flavored almond paste and vanilla icing — but be forewarned, it's becoming hard to find). Another ode to vanilla, a central ingredient of good pastry: the Grand Cru Vanille, whose sublimely white matte surface conceals a charcoal black heart at its center (a concentrate of vanilla), airy vanilla cream, crunchy almond, fleur de sel and vanilla bean. The first time I tried it, I felt like I was floating into heaven.

La Pâtisserie des Rêves? A magnificent universe created by Thierry Teyssier and pastry chef Philippe Conticini. Their cakes are almost architecturally structured around flavor and the pleasure it brings. Philippe Conticini goes so far as to speak of seasoning and 'condimentation' in pastry — he's a flavor genius! (See also page 102.)

Napoléon
Café Pouchkine

Piled high with fresh fruit (raspberry, strawberry, and blackberry), this vertiginously tall cake is closer to a viennoiserie. Concealed in its brioche pastry are fine caramelized layers that make it light and puffy, but also a delicate vanilla cream in the center. The Rose Pouchkine, with its white chocolate petals and golden leaves, its creamy center (with a strong bitter-almond flavor), its stewed fruit and pistachio biscuit, is aesthetically striking, though perhaps less impressive in taste.

Le Café Pouchkine? A Moscow-based shop which opened a corner stand inside the Printemps department store in 2012. Surrounded by gold, shimmering reflections and exuberant architectural details, the desserts are quite a spectacle in their display. The counter across the aisle where you can pause for a pastry or a hot chocolate draws a crowd (personally, I find the limited seating a little tight).

The Secret of the Finishing Touch
The velvety surface that coats many an entremets these days is obtained using a spray gun filled with a mix of cocoa butter, melted white chocolate, and food coloring. This technique produces a nice matte, powdered effect.

For addresses, see page 121.

♥ Kashmir
Des Gâteaux & Du Pain

Warm, enchanting notes of saffron, orange-and-date compote, and almond biscuit: this simple-looking cake (a pretty saffron-colored dome) elegantly combines flavors rarely found these days in pastries. The first bite transports me to the Spice Road, and I allow myself to be swept away. The mango-caramel spiced Saint-Honoré likewise evokes tart flavors and rich sensations with its soft choux pastry, sablé cookie and smooth caramel whipped cream. Continuing the mouth-watering theme of exotic fruit and tart notes, the Lipstick combines lemon cream, lemon zest, and pineapple compote on a crunchy almond-brown sugar crust.

Des Gâteaux & Du Pain? The pastries of Claire Damon, one of the few women in the profession in Paris, are extremely well thought-out and irremediably seductive. I know that some people feel ill at ease in this tiny shop, with its black walls and its desserts displayed like little gems, but it is well worth overcoming any initial apprehension.

♥ Pomme Yuzu Macaron
Sébastien Dégardin, Pâtisserie du Panthéon

An excellent, slightly sticky (as it should be) macaron shell topped with apples "coufides". Coufides? Apples baked for 8 hours until meltingly confit. The result is incomparable. A layer of yuzu pulp cream lies between the apple and the macaron shell. (The yuzu is a Japanese, mandarin-flavoured citrus fruit.) The contrasting textures superbly enhance the apple. Another lovely cake is the Passiflore with its extra-exotic notes: sitting on a thin, coconut shortbread biscuit is a passion fruit cream topped with a very light, white chocolate mousse. For lovers of the Paris-Brest, this one with lots of praline (a nougatine layer gracefully floats on top and its centre filled with pure praline cream), is worthy of being honoured in the Panthéon—just a few steps away from the patisserie.

Sébastien Dégardin, Pâtisserie du Panthéon? Former head pastry chef initially at Michel Troisgros' restaurant moved on to Pierre Gagnaire's establishment, before opening his own place in the 12th Arrondissement. At the end of 2013, he moved into and modernised this magnificent location where part of the decoration has been classified by the Monuments Historiques of France.

The Irresistible Pastry

When I look through a shop window, I sometimes feel as if certain desserts are calling me, reaching out to me, doing everything in their power to draw me in. I don't think it's just my imagination. With their perfectly ripe fruit, their bright, fiery caramel, their thick chocolate shavings, or their endlessly voluptuous mounds of cream, pastries can become true objects of desire.

For addresses, see page 121.

1. Inside one of the Des Gâteaux et du Pain locations
2. The display case at Des Gâteaux et du Pain
3. The mille-feuille at Des Gâteaux et du Pain
4. The Passiflore by Sébastien Dégardin at the Pâtisserie du Panthéon
5. Inside Sébastien Dégardin's boutique, the Pâtisserie du Panthéon

1. The Victor Caramel at Hugo & Victor
2. The Hugo Combawa at Hugo & Victor
3. Inside Hugo & Victor
4. The Hugo Amande at Hugo & Victor
5. The Trousseau at Blé Sucré
6. Inside Blé Sucré

Hugo Vanille
Hugo & Victor

In this dome of layered creams, the vanilla is omnipresent, instantly satisfying the desires of vanilla aficionados such as myself. The salted butter caramel mille-feuille is another must (with a center of pure caramel hidden inside the cream). Depending on the season, blood orange, rhubarb, lemongrass, verbena, or pomegranate (flavors we rarely see in pastry, which — I admit — I have a weakness for) appear in different forms and give rise to beautiful creations. Like the Hugo Orange Sanguine, which plays marvelously with crispy and creamy textures, with the sweetness of white chocolate and the bitterness of blood orange.

Hugo & Victor? A shop that displays its creations in glass cases along the walls might be a little disconcerting. But for the duo formed by Hugues Pouget and Sylvain Blanc, it's a conscious decision to lure customers into a kind of 'cabinet of sweet curiosities'. (See also page 69.)

Trousseau
Blé Sucré

Underneath this smooth, shiny dome lies a creamy, milky chocolate mousse (I'm guessing about the milk chocolate) on a thin cocoa-flavored biscuit base, the whole thing covered with slightly tart raspberry icing. Though it might be overdone, raspberry and (milk?) chocolate is always a perfect combination, there's no doubt about it! Also dome-shaped, the Vollon holds its own with another consistently good combination of flavors: a mousse-like, intense dark chocolate cream, with an unexpected bit of vanilla cream in the center, all sitting on a crunchy praline and almond dacquoise.

Blé Sucré? A small neighborhood shop created by Fabrice Le Bourdat. A veteran of Michelin-starred restaurants, this pastry chef creates beautiful new desserts alongside delicious staples (I hear through the grapevine that you must try the salted butter caramel religieuse and the financier).

A Luxurious Decor
Walls painted black or highlighted in gold, glass domes or jewelry cases for displaying the cakes, sales staff in designer uniforms: today's pastry chefs spare no expense when it comes to creating an atmosphere of luxury, elegance, and sophistication.

For addresses, see page 121.

♥ *Sweet Burger*
Chez Bogato

You read it right, this is a pastry version of a burger and the resemblance is indeed a bit jarring. It is as delicious as it is amusing: two almond-flavored macaron shells for the bun, a thick layer of intense dark chocolate ganache for the patty, a thin yellow square of almond paste for the cheese, a crushed-raspberry sauce for the ketchup, and a mint leaf for the lettuce: to be eaten joyfully with your fingers! The chocolate Denfert tart (with a strongly cocoa-flavored ganache), decorated with a mini-skull and some sesame nougatine, is also excellent. The Chalala, with its madeleine cake, raspberry-rose pastry cream, and little almond paste bow, is decidedly more coquettish and also turns out to be quite a treat.

Chez Bogato? A shop opened by Anaïs Olmer, who went from advertising to dessert creation, making everything from very large cakes to order to bite-sized treats to go. All the candies of our childhood are here and the cakes and cookies seem to be designed with magic. You'll find everything from humor to poetry in this mouthwatering den of sweet surprises. (See also page 119.)

Lola
Arnaud Larher

On a perfect sablé crust, the velvety, tart passion fruit cream (Lord knows I love passion fruit!) sits on a raspberry jam that gives even more of a boost to the passion fruit, in an alchemy that only the chef knows how to create. The lemon tart (tarte au citron), with its cloud of beaten egg whites (like those in an île flottante, but not cooked) punctuated with clear yellow rounds, is as pretty to look at as it is delicious to eat. The praline mille-feuille is another excellent choice. Overall, you'll find as many innovative pastries as classics.

Arnaud Larher? Specializing in both pastries and chocolates, this Meilleur Ouvrier de France has mastered them equally well. As a result the chocolate pastries are superb, as are his classic desserts and his new creations. In short, it's all good! (See also pages 36 and 66.)

Traviata
La Maison du Chocolat

This dome has it all: shine, curves, and flavors that come together in perfect harmony! On the outside, a strongly cocoa-flavored icing, under which we find an excellent chocolate sabayon, concealing a Bourbon vanilla crème brûlée heart. At its base, an old-fashioned praline and an almond and hazelnut dacquoise add crunch and another layer of pure indulgence. Listen — I can hear Verdi's opera!

La Maison du Chocolat? In this temple of chocolate founded by Robert Linxe in 1977, where the creative director, Nicolas Cloiseau, accomplishes marvels of both classicism and creativity, pastries also have their moment. They are mostly chocolate-based, of course, but not only: the caramel and coffee éclairs are also very popular. (See also page 74.)

For addresses, see page 121.

1. Pastries at Chez Bogato
2. Arnaud Larher's Paradis
3. Pastries at Arnaud Larher
4. The Traviata at La Maison du Chocolat
5. Inside La Maison du Chocolat

1. Inside Pain de Sucre
2. Verrines at Pain de Sucre
3. The Pirouette tart at Pain de Sucre
4. The caramel tart and entremets at Sadaharu Aoki
5. Inside Sadaharu Aoki

♥ *Green Party*
Pain de Sucre

Creamy pistachio mousse with a light rosemary flavor, a rhubarb pulp center, and a soft cake base: I love the balance it strikes and the idea of adding a hint of an aromatic herb to a dessert. The Fleur de Sureau is another nice creation, made with strawberries and flowers: a few wild strawberries on top, an elderflower-flavored strawberry cream, crushed strawberries in the middle, and a crunchy sablé crust on the bottom. There are also more traditional fruit tarts, like the Pirouette, which combines raspberries, lime, and pistachio like you've never tasted. Worth noting: the row of little tables along the side of the shop on the rue Rambuteau is a lovely spot for a pastry break any time of day.

Pain de Sucre? Nathalie Robert and Didier Mathray met at the pastry station working for Michelin-starred chef Pierre Gagnaire before opening their own shop, where they perpetuate their unique approach to pastries. The result is beyond reproach: everything looks good! (See also page 80.)

Matcha Azuki
Sadaharu Aoki

An entremets combining matcha (Japanese green tea) and azuki (Japanese red beans). While its architecture evokes that of a French pastry, with its rectangular form and its different layers of cream and cake, the strong flavors of green tea and red bean are a sublime evocation of Japan, sitting, nonetheless, on a base of crunchy praline that brings you back to France. The other pastry that I adore here is the caramel tart (tarte au caramel). With its delicate sablé crust, its insane layer of salted caramel (the slightly thick and sticky kind), and its fine milk chocolate mousse on top, this tart is devilish!

Sadaharu Aoki? This Japanese pastry chef moved to France in 1991. His creations are inspired by great French classics, to which he adds a captivating Japanese touch. Among his favorite ingredients we find sesame, matcha, azuki beans, and even yuzu. (See also page 73.)

Japan in France
More and more Japanese chefs are opening restaurants in Paris these days, offering their own interpretation of French cuisine. The same is true of pastry: Japanese pastry chefs who open shops here often have a very classical vision, while at the same time introducing select Japanese ingredients in unique and daring ways.

For addresses, see page 121.

Baked Desserts

These cakes are different in that they are prepared not by a pastry chef, but by a baker. With a bit of yeast, a good batch of butter, and a lot of savoir-faire, these artisanal bakers are a big part of what brightens our early mornings (or snack times). Smelling the aroma of butter that fills the house, breaking off a piece of the best brioche in the world or dunking a top quality croissant in your coffee — let's face it, these are the incomparable pleasures of morning. Go on, whatever time it is, get your shoes on and get to the bakery!

Kouign-amann
Gontran Cherrier

Though it might look like raisin bread, its layered dough, caramelized crust, and intensely buttery aroma are not to be mistaken: this comes very close to the kouign-amann (which means 'butter cake' in Breton) we find in Brittany. If defenders of the 'authentic Douarnenez kouign-amann' heard me, they would answer that an individual size is an easy way out and that it comes nowhere near the savoir-faire of a Finistère baker (the standard kouign-amann weighs 600g). That said, it's the ideal size for a snack and its aroma of bread dough, butter, and caramel is pure heaven. The raisin bread and chocolate bread also hold their own quite well (with less butter, of course).

Gontran Cherrier? A baker who ventured quite a bit around France and abroad (restaurants, TV shows, cookbooks) before opening his own shop in Paris. His universe is inspired by his travels, and the bread recipes that he invents each season are astonishing. When it comes to viennoiseries, he has perfectly mastered their secrets.

Kouglof
Gérard Mulot

A light brioche that breaks apart easily (pulling apart in threads like cotton candy), plump raisins, and an incredible sensation when you bit into it: the crust is soaked in a syrup of almond, butter, and confectioner's sugar, Gérard Mulot's secret ingredient. This kouglof is sold by the kilo; it's up to you to choose the size. One piece of advice: don't hesitate to choose a bigger loaf than you had planned, so as not to be left empty-handed after everyone tears off their share!

Gérard Mulot? Originally from Vosges, Mulot moved to Saint-Germain-des-Prés in 1975. He is such a household name that if you ask the people in the neighborhood, I'm sure everyone will be able to tell you which dessert is their favorite. And among these, the kouglof has its fair share of fans. (See also page 11.)

Freshness!

Seduced by their buttery aroma, caramel color, and slightly flaky texture, I confess to having a weakness for the sweet baked goods we call viennoiseries. But if there's one thing that should be avoided, it's making them wait. Leftover croissants for breakfast? Never! By the following day, the croissant will have lost all of its charm and crunch — a totally unbearable thought!

For addresses, see page 121.

1. Inside Gontran Cherrier
2. Gontran Cherrier's *kouign-amann*
3. Different flavors of bread at Gontran Cherrier
4. *Kouglofs* and bread at Gérard Mulot
5. Baker-pastry chef Gérard Mulot

1. Horns of Bounty at Aki Boulangerie
2. The Melon Pan at Aki Boulangerie
3. Inside Aki Boulangerie
4. Baker-pastry chef Stéphane Vandermeersch
5. *Kouglofs* and pastries at
   Stéphane Vandermeersch

Matcha 'Melon'
Aki Boulangerie

This strongly green-tea-flavored milk bread filled with cubes of white chocolate makes for a decidedly exotic and indulgent snack. Is it called a 'melon' because of its spherical shape? Maybe. In any case, 'melon pan', or 'melon bread', is very common in Japan. The brioche bread shaped like a horn of plenty and filled with sweet red beans or yuzu cream is another interesting dessert that you just have to try.

Aki Boulangerie? Imagine French classics (bread and pastries) interpreted by a team of Japanese chefs, using a lot of green tea, sesame, rice paper, and azuki beans, and you have this unusual spot on the rue Saint Anne, where the bar-height tables and stools are never empty at lunchtime (the filling sandwiches are just as exotic).

♥ Kouglof
Stéphane Vandermeersch

One of this baker's stated specialties, it fills every corner of the bakery on the days it's made (Friday, Saturday, Sunday). We immediately understand why. The light and airy brioche, its edges soaked in syrup and covered with a dusting of sugar that adds a bit of crunch — this kouglof is one of the best I've ever tasted. With its beautiful spirals that form on top as it cooks, the Brioche Feuilletée is also quite enticing, not to mention the flavorful, ultra-crispy palmier, whose butter and caramel are reminiscent of a kouign-amann.

Stéphane Vandermeersch? A talented artisan who trained in feuilletage, or layering techniques, alongside Pierre Hermé, he has perfectly mastered its variants, like that of the pâte briochée. The shop (which is not very big) is warm and welcoming, with its spirit of tradition and 19th century decor still intact.

The Most Buttery Aroma?

The one escaping from the bags I brought home from Du Pain et Des Idées and La Gambette à Pain. Sitting in the metro, between the escargots, mounas, pains au chocolat, and sacristains, I thought I was going to start a riot. And it lasted all the way to my kitchen, where the aromas continued to fill the air and almost went to my head!

For addresses, see page 121.

Flan
Cyril Lignac

This eggless version is very refreshing. The milk-based batter is firm, with just the right amount of jiggle, and the very generous vanilla bean aroma completes this formidable and delicious monument. Note that the crust is made of puff pastry (not the usual short crust).

La Pâtisserie by Cyril Lignac? They also make bread and baked desserts. This eggless flan, a recipe developed with Benoît Couvrand, formerly of Fauchon, is sure to become the daily snack of everyone in the neighborhood (at least, it would be mine if I were in the area!). (See also page 12.)

Croissant
La Pâtisserie des Martyrs

Perfectly layered (the outside is divinely crispy, while the inside is soft and moist), an intoxicating aroma of butter, a touch of salt, a slight shine on the top that sticks to your fingers — this is one of my favorite croissants. I might add that when my daughter eats them, she smells deliciously like butter, which is a good sign, don't you think?

Sébastien Gaudard? For his first Paris shop, this son of a pastry chef from Lorraine said he wanted to 'give new life to pastries'. The most popular classics and many others taken from old recipe books are all there. The viennoiseries, particularly sophisticated and indulgent, are no exception. (See also pages 8 and 80.)

Praluline
Maison Pralus

A dense brioche, almost a brioche version of a gâche and, above all, full of bits of pink praline, caramelized on the outside and soft and melting on the inside (leaving just the crunch of the hazelnut and almond, always an excellent quality). The first time I ever tasted a Praluline in Roanne, it was like discovering a work of art. When you look at the inside, the pink layers are reminiscent of Jackson Pollock-type splatters. You can imagine how excited I was when I learned they were coming to Paris!

Maison Pralus? Loyal to the spirit of his grandfather, inventor of the Praluline in Roanne (Loire) in 1955, chocolatier François Pralus continues the tradition with this pink-streaked and positively addictive brioche. (See also page 56.)

The Case of Flan

This baked dessert fell out of fashion for a while, after customers tired of the rubbery industrial versions that flooded the market. Rest assured, however: conscientious bakers and pastry chefs are restoring its prestige with fresh, flavorful, generous flans.

For addresses, see page 121.

1. The *flan* at La Pâtisserie by Cyril Lignac
2. *Kouglofs* and *viennoiseries* at
   La Pâtisserie des Martyrs
3. Maison Pralus
4. The Praluline at Maison Pralus

1. Baker Christophe Vasseur of Du Pain et des Idées, with *mounas* and *escargots*
2. *Escargots* at Du Pain et des Idées
3. Cocoa bread and *viennoiseries* at Maison Landemaine
4. *Viennoiseries* at Maison Landemaine

🩶 *Fromage Blanc and Blueberry Escargot*
La Gambette à Pain

In the spiral of this high quality puff pastry escargot (pinwheel pastry) the flavors of butter, fruit, and cream spin delectably around. Also worth noting are the pistachio and chocolate versions, and the slice of mouna (a recipe originating in Algiers), one of the best brioches I know. Dense and deliciously flavored with orange peels, it fills the room with its aroma.

La Gambette à Pain? Chef Jean-Paul Mathon understands full well the air of sweet gluttony that should fill a bakery. I dare anyone to leave his shop with only a loaf of bread (the viennoiseries are each more enticing than the next).

Sacristain
Du Pain et Des Idées

This palmier dough filled with pastry cream twists around itself with enough crunch and happiness to go around. The pink praline escargot (a pinwheel of leavened puff pastry) is another great snack. Not to mention the mouna: with its compact dough subtly flavored with orange blossom, its dark crust, and its unobtrusive grains of sugar, it is a journey all its own.

Du Pain et Des Idées? The quality of its products is as much to be admired as its historical decor. Many of the baker Christophe Vasseur's recipes are similar to those of his mentor Jean-Paul Mathon, of La Gambette à Pain. I won't begin to try to tell the difference, but if you'd like to give it a shot...?

Pain au Cacao
Maison Landemaine

A traditional bread dough flavored with cocoa powder, but also filled with tons of bittersweet chocolate chips that melt a little as they cook. This bread could be my breakfast or my daily snack, if I could manage to not finish it before I even walk in my door (on the way somewhere, at any hour, it's a real treat to munch on). From the chausson aux pommes (an apple turnover filled with vanilla-flavored applesauce) to the croissant (crispy on the outside and soft and moist on the inside), the viennoiseries are also excellent.

Maison Landemaine? The talented bakers Rodolphe Landemaine and his Japanese-born wife Yoshimi have already taken over seven shops in Paris (and are surely not finished) and have opened a school in Tokyo. They're unstoppable!

For addresses, see page 121.

♥ Brioche Vendéenne
L'Autre Boulange

One of the most flavorful brioches I know! You have to love the aromas of butter, orange, and orange blossom, and the very compact dough that melts delectably in your mouth. This shop is also renowned for its flan, which is quite sweet and creamy, with a short crust (pâte brisée), a fine example of its kind. Among the viennoiseries, take a trip to North America by trying the pecan puff pastry filled with maple syrup.

L'Autre Boulange? With a warm, old-fashioned welcome from staff who say all the right things, the bakehouse and oven visible from the entrance, good breads and good viennoiseries made by Denis Durand, this shop reminds me of the bakeries of my childhood. It's just the kind we would all like to have right down the street.

Pain au Chocolat aux Amandes
Mori Yoshida

Only for lovers of this particular pastry; it might be too much for the rest of you. This artisanal baker doesn't hesitate to 'stuff' a good chocolate croissant with plenty of almond paste. A nice layer of almond paste on top, almond paste inside, and we have a very filling — as you might imagine — and very indulgent snack.

Mori Yoshida? This Japanese pastry chef has taken on all aspects of French artisanship — baking included, of course — with very, very satisfying results. (See also page 15.)

Pain au Chocolat
Dominique Saibron

Simple, but very well executed, this pain au chocolat will brighten your Sunday morning, as will the croissant from the same shop. Delicate layers, buttery but not overly so, and — an important detail, you must admit — the double bar of chocolate inside is of excellent quality. If you're really hungry, take a look at or a bite of the pistachio tournicotis (a kind of escargot filed with pistachio-flavored cream and dusted with bits of crushed pistachio), whose generous size will fill you up for the day.

Dominique Saibron? A baker known on the Rive Gauche since 1987, who made a bigger name for himself by opening a shop in Japan in 2008. He then returned to Paris, on the place d'Alésia, and his storefront hasn't been empty since.

For addresses, see page 121.

1. The Brioche Vendéenne at L'Autre Boulange
2. Pain au Chocolat aux Amandes at Mori Yoshida
3. Baker Dominique Saibron
4. Viennoiseries at Dominique Saibron

Chocolate

I love it in all its forms and ever since a certain trip
to Ecuador, I feel like I know it a little more intimately.
To meet producers, cross the cacao tree forests in a jeep,
watch the pods fall, and smell the beans as they ferment
— it was like a sweet dream coming true. But back to our
tastings. In my opinion, there are many different, satisfying
ways to enjoy chocolate: bars, bonbons, and other
chocolate treats.

1. Patrick Roger's pastry shop
2. Inside Patrick Roger
3. A box of chocolates at Patrick Roger
4. Unconched chocolate bars at La Manufacture
   de Chocolat d'Alain Ducasse
5. La Manufacture de Chocolat d'Alain Ducasse

Chocolate Bars

Affordable and always within reach, chocolate bars are an easy way to have a little bit of chocolate every day. And, in my opinion, a hand-crafted bar made from the highest quality cocoa is unparalleled.

Indonesie
Patrick Roger

Sensitive souls beware, the extremely tart and smoky notes in this dark chocolate (78% cocoa) might be disturbing, causing strong, assuredly exotic sensations. I insist on the fact that this is not a bar to put in just any hands! If you are looking for something sweeter, with hazelnuts, try the Praliné. The first time I heard of it, I thought it sounded like a deluge of sensations for lovers of praline. I can confirm: it is a vertiginous dose of little grains (of sugar and roasted hazelnuts), crunchiness, caramelized and hazelnut flavors, all covered in dark or milk chocolate (both are available).

Patrick Roger? This Meilleur Ouvrier de France does not go unnoticed in the world of chocolate. His acute sense of aesthetics led him to choose the colors of his boxes to better showcase the chocolate. And in the windows, he displays animals (gorillas, bears) that he sculpts in chocolate and that are so expressive you would swear they were alive! (See also page 74.)

♥ Unconched Chocolate Bar
La Manufacture de Chocolat d'Alain Ducasse

Conching, or refining, is the final step in the chocolate making process. Without it, imagine a raw chocolate whose ingredients have not come together yet, taking us back to the origins of the cocoa itself. Barely have you opened the packaging when the aromas burst intensely forth. In your mouth, you can feel the sugar crackling under your teeth, all the ingredients separating out so that you can taste the particularity of each: cacao beans, sugar, milk (for milk chocolate). The dark chocolate version is different, foregrounding the flavor of the cacao bean even more. This chocolate is a bit off-putting at first, before quickly becoming addictive.

La Manufacture de Chocolat d'Alain Ducasse? What Alain Ducasse wants, the king of French gastronomy gets. He had always dreamed of making chocolate, so he and his executive pastry chef, Nicolas Berger, opened a workshop in 2013, La Manufacture de Chocolat. What a treat to find chocolate hand-crafted in Paris! (See also page 62.)

For addresses, see page 121.

♥ *Melissa Bar*
Maison Pralus

Forty-five percent cocoa is high for milk chocolate, and you can taste it in the first bite. It has a nice length on the palate, with notes of honey and caramel: in my opinion, it's one of the best milk chocolates around. The other delight at Maison Pralus is the Galet Chuao, a dark chocolate made from a Venezuelan cacao bean — intense, subtle, best tasted in this ideal, thin format. There is also the São Tomé bar, a slightly tart variety of cocoa, delicately roasted and ground up with bits of cacao bean, and the Barre Infernale au Lait (milk chocolate filled with very flavorful praline and whole roasted hazelnuts). Not to mention those little marble-sized balls of chocolate, which could be filed under 'chocolate treats': like a Malteser, but crunchier, more delicate inside, and on the outside, the house milk chocolate. You can imagine the result.

Maison Pralus? François Pralus is one of the rare chocolatiers in France to produce bean-to-bar chocolate. His bars made with cocoa harvested in the four corners of the world are up there with the richest, most indulgent chocolates, the kind that almost make you feel like a kid again. (See also page 46.)

Fresh Fruit Bar
Jean-Charles Rochoux

It's only made on Saturday and Sunday, so you'll have to plan ahead (and call in the morning to have some put aside). What you get is a chocolate bar chock full of fresh seasonal fruit. In June, flavorful raspberries are covered in dark chocolate, without requiring a thick layer. This is a refined, refreshing bar that you have to eat within 48 hours — as if you could go longer than that! If you take a look at the so-called 'classic' bars, you'll see that they are sourced in many different countries, inviting you on a delectable voyage around the world.

Jean-Charles Rochoux? Having trained under Michel Chaudun (7th arrondissement), whose influence is noticeable, this artisan knows how to mold chocolate into infinite variations, including bars and spreads, not to mention his realistic animals. Worth noting, the silver bag with the crocodile-skin relief that we take away with our order is utterly chic!

The Sound of a Chocolate Bar

It might be the simplest form of chocolate, in appearance at least, but for me it is one of the most pleasurable. Even before you get to the aroma and the taste, there's the sound. At the snap of the first square breaking off, my ears perk up and my taste buds stand at attention!

For addresses, see page 121.

1. Chocolate bars
   at Jean-Charles Rochoux

2. A Maison Pralus
   Mélissa bar

3. Chocolate bar pyramids
   at Maison Pralus

4. Jean-Charles Rochoux

5. Assorted chocolate
   bars by
   Jean-Charles Rochoux

1. A box of chocolates at Pierre Marcolini
2. Chocolate bars at Pierre Marcolini
3. Inside Pierre Marcolini
4. A box of chocolates at Franck Kestener
5. Inside Franck Kestener
6. Atlantique chocolate bars at Franck Kestener

Rios Ecuador Bar
Pierre Marcolini

This dark chocolate (78% cocoa), made with beans from the Hacienda Puerto Romero, owned by Pedro Martinetti, is dear to my heart, and how could it be otherwise? I was following Pierre Marcolini when I visited Mr. Martinetti's plantation in 2010. For this bar, Ecuadorian Nacional beans are used. Planters have nicknamed its flavor 'arriba', for its origins 'up the river', which translates into very pleasant notes of fruit. With its frank tartness and its share of mystery, this chocolate brings me back to the brightly colored cacao pods, agile machete-wielding workers, and intensely humid heat — an emotional memory.

Pierre Marcolini? This Belgian chocolatier is one of the rare artisans to manufacture his own chocolate. Traveling regularly to visit the plantations, he absorbs the differences in terroir and tries to transcribe them as faithfully as possible in his bars.

Atlantique Bar
Franck Kestener

At first glance, it looks like a very classic chocolate bar. But under its fine outer layer of dark chocolate lies the epitome of the sablé (with just the right amount of butter and brittleness) and a sea salt caramel the likes of which you have no idea. This snack will transport you straight to the Atlantic shores of Brittany.

Franck Kestener? This Meilleur Ouvrier de France based in Sarreguemines in Lorraine has rather discreetly opened up a shop in Paris, but it has everything it needs to make us come back for more.

A Question of Origin

With single origin chocolate bars (that is, made with cocoa from a single country or region), chocolatiers try to transcribe the unique flavor of a specific climate and soil. Depending on the origin, the chocolate can plunge your senses into a tropical rainforest or warm soil, or bring out fruity or smoky notes. There's quite a large range of possibilities! The chocolatier Stéphane Bonnat knows exactly how to put that into words on the back of his bars.

For addresses, see page 121.

1. The butter caramel chocolate bar by Zotter at ChocoLatitudes
2. Inside ChocoLatitudes
3. L'Arbre à Café
4. Claudio Corallo's chocolate bars at L'Arbre à Café

♥ Butter Caramel Bar
Zotter at ChocoLatitudes

From an Austrian organic fair-trade brand, this chocolate bar filled with two layers of caramel will take you to new heights of ecstasy. The first layer is a cream studded with bits of crunchy caramel, while the second is a rather thick, salty, English toffee-type butter caramel, the whole thing wrapped in milk chocolate. One bite and you're a goner. For lovers of raw chocolate (that is, from unroasted beans), Zotter has an exquisitely fresh bar made of 80% cocoa. Laurence Alemanno has also selected bars of rare cocoa varieties from Bonnat (a chocolatier in Voiron, in Isère). Don't miss the one made from Mexican Real Del Xoconuzco cocoa (which comes from one of the oldest cacao trees in the world), a bar of unprecedented unctuousness, whose chocolate flavor will make you cry.

ChocoLatitudes? At Laurence Alemanno's shop, we come to nourish ourselves with values (diversity, organic agriculture, fair trade), knowledge, and total indulgence. Filled with objects, books, bars, and other chocolate products, her shop is a never-ending source of pleasure and discovery. (See also page 119.)

♥ 73% Bar with Cacao Nibs
Claudio Corallo at L'Arbre à Café

Put your nose in the bag and you'll understand. Its aroma is that of the workshop, of noble, raw materials. Now taste: it's a return to the beans, to the source, a freshness and an interminable length on the palate, and of course, a light crackling under the teeth at times from the nibs. The taste lingers in your mouth even when the silky chocolate has disappeared. There you are: as close as you can get to the bean and to a grand moment of flavor.

Claudio Corallo? This Italian-born artisan cultivates cacao in São Tomé and Príncipe, the second smallest country in Africa, formed by two islands on the equator in the Gulf of Guinea. He uses only the cocoa he produces, cocoa butter, and sugar to produce his chocolate, with no additives (such as vanilla or soy lecithin). In Paris, his chocolate is distributed by L'Arbre à Café.

For addresses, see page 121.

Chocolate Bonbons

It's the professional term for what we commonly call chocolats in France and pralines in Belgium. A box of chocolates is usually composed of three categories of bonbons: praline, pure ganache, and flavored ganache. In my mind the ideal box is like a good novel that you can't wait to get back into.

♥ Pralines
La Manufacture de Chocolat d'Alain Ducasse

Be forewarned, these are among the best I have ever had in my life! Peanut butter (unusual), pistachio (in a quite salty version), hazelnut: the nutty flavors are extremely well transcribed. And to make them even more stimulating, they are available in different textures, from very crunchy to soft and melting. It's worth getting a box of these alone — luckily, you can!

La Manufacture de Chocolat d'Alain Ducasse? In their Manufacture de Chocolat in Paris, the duo of Alain Ducasse and Nicolas Berger manufacture chocolate from the bean itself, but also make their own pralines by roasting and caramelizing nuts, then grinding them, to incomparable result (many chocolatiers use ready-made praline). (See also page 55.)

Flavored Ganache
Jacques Genin

With their thin and lightly crisp coating, when they are smoothed between the tongue and the palate, it takes only a few instants for ganache (mostly made of dark chocolate) to exude the flavor it has been infused with. I have a weakness for mint and basil ganaches, which express all the fullness these fresh herbs can take on inside the chocolate. Coffee, vanilla (with its slightly crunchy seeds), and 'sweet' spices also come through quite well. I should add that the pralines have the same texture as the ganaches, that is, smooth and creamy (personally, I prefer them crunchy).

Jacques Genin? With his laboratory set up in the heart of the Marais, this chocolatier pushes the quest for quality quite far and knows how to fill each of his bonbons with a delicate touch. (See also pages 83 and 98.)

Secrets of Texture
What gives pralines a lot of crunch is the addition of crêpe dentelle. Broken down into shards, it adds crunch to any fatty substance into which it is incorporated.

For addresses, see page 121.

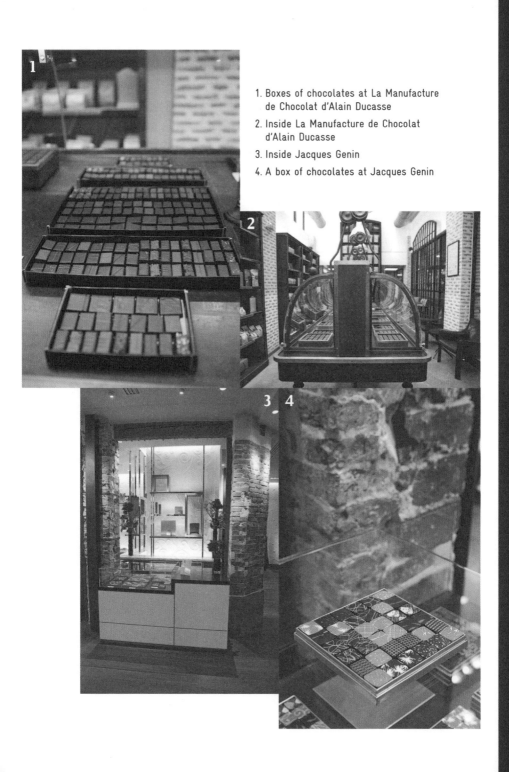

1. Boxes of chocolates at La Manufacture de Chocolat d'Alain Ducasse
2. Inside La Manufacture de Chocolat d'Alain Ducasse
3. Inside Jacques Genin
4. A box of chocolates at Jacques Genin

1. A box of chocolates at Le Cacaotier
2. The window at Le Cacaotier
3. Inside Pierre Hermé
4. Chocolates at Pierre Hermé

Bonbons
Le Cacaotier

These generous cubes have us sinking our teeth in with great enthusiasm. The pralines — like the Speculoos with its nice biscuit flavor, the Crumble with its continuous crunch, or the Bourgogne with its bits of nougat — are divine. In dark or milk chocolate, the Farinelli is stunning with its tender salted butter caramel ganache. As for the dark chocolate ganache varieties, they are severely intense; I have a weakness for the Extra Bitter made from Venezuelan cocoa, which lingers for a long time on the palate. I can't help but also mention the diabolical milk chocolate bar with very, very crunchy almonds (It's sold by the kilo and it's best to break yourself off a big piece!).

Le Cacaotier? After a voyage around the world (Guatemala, London, Australia), the chocolatier Hubert Masse opened his first shop in France at Enghien-les-Bains, in Val d'Oise. He uses only the finest raw materials and his creations are seasonally poetic (I love the chocolate autumn leaves).

 Bonbons
Pierre Hermé

Each one is an adventure which, if you close your eyes, will transport you far away: to the heat of Mexico with the Tsuki and its crunchy praline with bits of roasted, salted corn and a hint of orange; or across time to the world of the Vikings with the bittersweet chocolate and smoked-salt butter ganache of the daring Nuage; as for the Infiniment Vanille and its ganache infused with vanilla from Tahiti, Mexico, and Madagascar, which I can still feel crunching under my teeth, it's a pure vanilla high.

Pierre Hermé? We know him for his immense talent as a pastry chef, perhaps less so for his sharp sense of chocolate, and yet. Just like his pastries, each one of his bonbons is a creation unto itself, a very special harmony. (See also page 28.)

Individual Bonbons

Before leaving the shop, be sure that you have a list of what is inside your box of chocolates. When you taste the bonbons, this can help answer questions about a flavor that you can't quite define (which can be very annoying). Chocolatiers are not shy about exploring new domains of flavor (rare spices, herbs, flowers, exotic or unexpected fruits), and they don't hesitate to combine flavors that are not always easy to distinguish.

For addresses, see page 121.

Bonbons
Arnaud Larher

A marvelously executed standard is what I think as I taste these chocolates one by one. The thin, wide square is a very pleasant shape that you can nibble bit by bit, mounting to a crescendo of flavor. The fine, flavorful ganache can be surprising, like the astonishing dark chocolate ganache infused with wild peppercorns. The praline is also excellent: the pistachio flavor has a light crunch and the sesame and coconut are among the most surprising.

Arnaud Larher? Open in Montmartre for the past 15 years, this Meilleur Ouvrier de France is one of the rare artisans to handle both pastries and chocolates with equal skill. His fine, classic chocolates are a sure bet. (See also pages 33 and 66.)

Bonbons
Jean-Paul Hévin

With their rather thick format (which gives them a bit of chew), these chocolates explode generously in your mouth. Intensely flavorful but also quite refined, they alternate between identifiable flavors and mysterious notes, like the stunning Gemme with its dark chocolate ganache macerated in smoked Chinese tea or the indulgent Anapurna with its duo of chestnut paste and milk chocolate mousse. The pure ganaches reveal the chocolatier's talent for translating all of the facets of cocoa, from the slightly tart Cao to the bitter Caribbean variety.

Jean-Paul Hévin? Like a fashion designer, this chocolatier and Meilleur Ouvrier de France develops beautiful, smooth, shiny or rough materials for each of his bonbons, creating sublime textures and flavors. You can see that he has understood all of the subtleties of chocolate. (See also page 101.)

Meilleur Ouvrier de France

The MOF title is obtained through a competition among the most formidable artisans (in efficiency, speed, perfection), is kept for life, and, incidentally, grants the right to attach the blue-white-and-red collar to one's jacket. Established in 1924, the competition takes place every four years in the different food professions: cooking, pastry-confectionary, bakery, wine, produce, butchery, ice cream, cheese, and fish.

For addresses, see page 121.

1. Inside Arnaud Larher
2. Pastry chef-chocolatier Arnaud Larher
3. Inside Jean-Paul Hévin
4. Chocolates at Jean-Paul Hévin

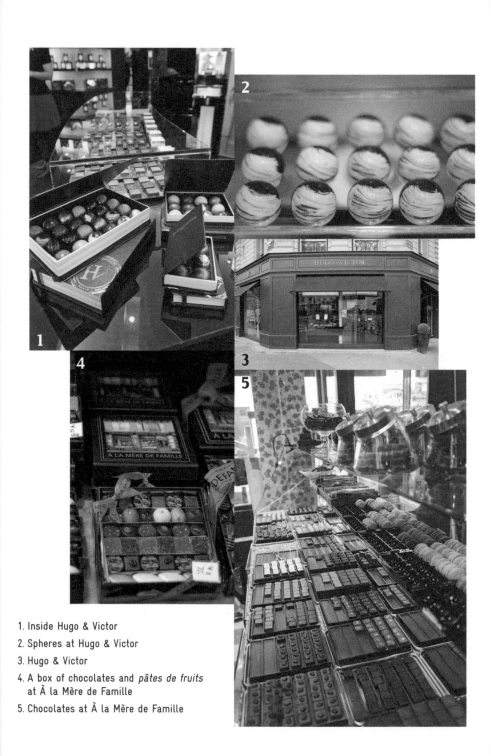

1. Inside Hugo & Victor
2. Spheres at Hugo & Victor
3. Hugo & Victor
4. A box of chocolates and *pâtes de fruits* at À la Mère de Famille
5. Chocolates at À la Mère de Famille

Spheres
Hugo & Victor

Half spheres, actually. A fine dark or milk chocolate shell filled with a thick caramel, whose very concentrated flavor varies according to the season: lemongrass, passion fruit, or verbena in the spring, chestnut, apple, or pomegranate in the fall. To differentiate the flavors, the shells are decorated with paint brush strokes, dots, or touches of gold. The Spheres are sold in little boxes shaped like black books with a golden title. You need only open the cover to admire its contents. Very chic!

Hugo & Victor? In this 'cabinet of sweet curiosities', founded by Hugues Pouget and Sylvain Blanc, the art of pastries is handled with brio, but the Spheres are also worth the detour. (See also page 35.)

♥ Bonbons
À la Mère de Famille

Walnuts, coffee ganache, and nougatine: it doesn't sound like much listed like that, yet this crunchy, crispy chocolate that melts into its complementary flavors is a little morsel of happiness. The pralines are also excellent; there is the sesame version with hints of halva (the confection found around the Mediterranean basin) and those that combine hazelnut and almond are very crunchy. The half-spheres of coconut add an element of surprise. One final detail: when I compose a box myself, I can't help but add a few Florentines (I love them!). Let me add that these bonbons are among the least expensive of this chapter.

À la Mère de Famille? A centuries-old institution of confectionary whose original shop on the Faubourg-Montmartre is worth going to see. Today, its legacy is carried on brilliantly through the creativity of its chef, Julien Merceron, and the dynamism of its owners, the Dolfi family. Parisians and tourists alike rush to this shop, myself included! (See also page 92.)

Careful! Conserve Well!

Never put a box of chocolates or a chocolate bar in the refrigerator — the cold irremediably 'breaks' the aromas. The risk of losing all of the nuances and subtleties intended by the artisan is too great. Out of respect for him and for your chocolates, avoid the cold!

For addresses, see page 121.

Bonbons
Christophe Roussel

With a few flavors from Brittany, and a touch of humor and inventiveness, this chocolatier originally from La Baule creates charming, delicate chocolate. The Kisses From (shaped like a pair of sensual red lips), with its hints of raspberry and its crunchy pearls, is irresistible. I also like the Guérande with its soft caramel cooked with sea salt and flavored with vanilla, the Tahiti and its praline that deftly combines almond, hazelnut, and coconut, and the Tiramisu, with its cakey texture and its refined note of coffee.

Christophe Roussel? This renowned pastry chef-chocolatier from La Baule, in Loire-Atlantique, now has two shops in Paris. One is in the Hôtel du Cadran, near the rue Cler, and is decorated with the hotel's gray tones. The other, a stand-alone shop at the foot of Sacré-Coeur, is a better reflection of the artisan's colors and spirit.

Bonbons
Henri Le Roux

A lot of dark chocolate, ingredients from Brittany, and Japanese flavors: these very delicate chocolates are truly an invitation to a voyage. The Soizig with its crumbled buckwheat praline deliciously sings of Brittany. The Praliné à la Courge uses roasted pumpkin seeds, seasoned with a dash of sea salt, which give it an insane amount of flavor. As for the matcha (green tea) flavored white chocolate ganache with raspberry fruit paste, I fantasize about having a box of these alone.

Henri Le Roux? Originally a 'caramélier' in Quiberon, Henri Le Roux made a name for himself with his famous salted butter caramels (caramel au beurre salé, or CBS) and his chocolates (Soizig, Truffe de Truffe). The Japanese company which took over in 2006 remained faithful to the spirit of the master, with a few welcome Japanese touches. (See also page 84.)

For addresses, see page 121.

1. Tiramisu chocolate at Christophe Roussel
2. Kisses at Christophe Roussel
3. Christophe Roussel
4. Inside Henri Le Roux
5. Chocolates at Henri Le Roux

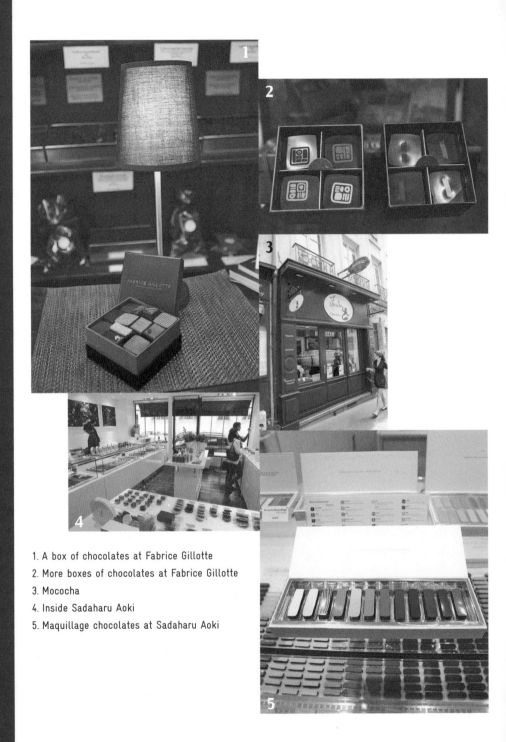

1. A box of chocolates at Fabrice Gillotte
2. More boxes of chocolates at Fabrice Gillotte
3. Mococha
4. Inside Sadaharu Aoki
5. Maquillage chocolates at Sadaharu Aoki

♥ *Bonbons at Mococha*
Fabrice Gillotte

Some of the most imaginative and audacious bonbons I've seen. Ganache, gelée, praline — the chocolatier superimposes textures, uses unexpected ingredients, and creates new sensations without hesitation. Among the nut flavors, the Muscovado leans towards a hazelnut praline flavor, which is prolonged by the muscovado sugar and its hint of licorice. Of the Provencal flavors, the Lavande, with its tender lavender honey nougatine covered in dark chocolate, is a sublime homage to flowers and honey. The Aquacao contains a very intense dark chocolate ganache and a gelée made from water infused with cacao beans. Not to mention Couleurs de Bourgogne, a collection of ganaches and gelées of regional fruits (vineyard peach, raspberry, blackcurrant).

Fabrice Gillotte? Based in Dijon, this Meilleur Ouvrier de France focuses his work on discovering new sensations that chocolate can procure. In Paris, the Mococha shop distributes some of his creations (to my great delight).

Bonbons Maquillage
Sadaharu Aoki

These chocolates shaped like little fingers come in 18 different colors and flavors, which make the box look like a palette of makeup. With a bright color on top of a dark chocolate coating and ganache on the inside, they all have the same structure, except that the 18 different flavors are not just names. Each ganache is intensely flavored, whether it be with rose, yuzu (a mandarin-like Japanese citrus), green tea, or candied orange. You'll quickly fall in love with their flowery or fruity flavors, delicacy, and pretty packaging!

Sadaharu Aoki? The Japanese pastry chef-chocolatier Aoki arrived in Paris in 1991 to learn French pastry, bringing with him his own way of working with chocolates, which are always beautifully designed and very colorful. (See also page 39.)

The Salon du Chocolat

This annual convention brings together the best chocolatiers in the country with others from around the world. Here, you'll have the chance to discover other facets of cocoa and stock up on chocolate from Lyon (Bernachon), Nantes (Vincent Guerlais), Japan (Café Ozhan), or Vietnam (Marou). I admit it, I can't resist — I show up every year!

For addresses, see page 121.

Truffles and Other Chocolate Pleasures

Christmasy truffles, chocolate-covered nuts, and other tasty treats from the imagination of top artisans: here are a few guilty pleasures that just might turn into addictions.

Truffles
Patrick Roger

Perfectly round and covered in powdered cocoa as per tradition, here they reach the pinnacle of chocolatey flavor (with a blend of two different varieties of cocoa) and the melting softness that one expects from a truffle (thanks to a good dose of crème fraîche, apparently). Among the bonbons, I notice (and appreciate) a nice repertoire of tart notes that enhance the chocolate particularly well, such as lemon and basil ganache (the Delhi), Szechuan pepper ganache (the Macao), and half-spheres of caramel and lime (the Amazone). The orangettes, with their extra-large portion (made with real peel) and their delicious chew, are likewise monuments of their kind.

Patrick Roger? When he's developing his chocolates, it involves a whole process of assembly and a quest for the best ingredients. Each chocolate is its own unique creation. (See also page 55.)

The Cacao Bean Trend
I appreciate the way chocolatiers have been using crushed cacao beans, also known as nibs or 'grué'. I have to say that their crunchy texture and raw cocoa taste make them an alluring ingredient. Nibs can be blended into bars, bonbons, etc. or even eaten alone.

Gourmandises
La Maison du Chocolat

These little sticks of praliné moussé might seem like UFOs. Long and thin, made to be eaten with the tips of your fingers, they have a shape like nothing else we know. Hazelnut praline with bits of crêpe dentelle, almond and hazelnut praline with caramelized biscuits, almond praline with roasted, caramelized coconut: three flavors that express themselves with the utmost refinement and richness. I will, of course, also mention the bonbons, which are very traditional, extremely well executed, and unanimously appreciated (I was lucky enough to be offered a giant box of them for the birth of my daughter when I was still in the hospital — what a welcome surprise!).

La Maison du Chocolat? A temple dedicated to chocolate, founded by Robert Linxe in 1977. With the chef Nicolas Cloiseau (Meilleur Ouvrier de France), classics are revisited in just measure and the creations that grace the display throughout the year are cutting edge. (See also page 36.)

For addresses, see page 121.

1. Truffles and bonbons at Patrick Roger
2. and 3. Inside Patrick Roger
4. Maison du Chocolat's *Gourmandises*
5. Inside a Maison du Chocolat boutique

Grignotis
Régis

Bits of toasted almonds and pistachios, dried blueberries and raisins, candied orange peels, all covered in white, dark, or milk chocolate: the risk is that you finish the bag in less time than it takes to describe its contents. Roasted to add more crunch, soft where it counts, and all very flavorful, the fruits and nuts chosen for the Grignotis are of the highest quality. The more traditional chocolate bonbons are also well made, in particular the pralines, which add a variety of different textures (from the most melt-in-your-mouth to the crunchiest).

Régis? A well-known chocolate shop on the rue de Passy (16th arrondissement) for 50 years, where Gilles Daumoinx now dedicates his energy.

♥ Caramandes
Benoît Chocolats

These thin triangles can be deceptive. Wrapped in dark chocolate, the fine nougatine of slivered almonds embedded in salted caramel is tantalizingly crunchy and reminiscent of the flavors I loved as a child. You have to take little bites, but you won't be able to stop. The chocolate bonbons are just as indulgent, like the caramel or strawberry ganache, with its little seeds that crunch under your teeth. The bitter Concerto ganache is captivating and the mint variety makes your mouth feel like a refreshing cocoa-flavored garden. Made exclusively by Angers-based La Petite Marquise, Quernons d'Ardoise are also available. This exquisite Angers specialty made of thin nougatine covered in blue chocolate is more of a sweet confection.

Benoît Chocolats? The only woman chocolatier in this guide! Since taking over from her father, Gilbert, Anne-Françoise Benoît has let her creativity flow without hesitation (for example in the Concerto and Caramandes). While the original shop is in Angers, there are branches in Lille and Paris.

When to Say When?

It's hard to say. All these little chocolate creations are made to be popped into your mouth without thinking, in a gesture that you could repeat forever. It crumbles, melts, crunches, it's smooth — it's good. In other words, don't bother trying: it's impossible to stop!

For addresses, see page 121.

1. Chocolates at Régis
2. Inside Régis
3. Caramandes at Benoît Chocolats
4. Benoît Chocolats

Confectionery

Tender guimauves (marshmallow squares), sticky caramels, or tart fruit pastes — whether they are artisanal or, for that matter, industrially made (chocolate bars, caramels, marshmallows), sweets always have a joyous effect on our spirits. Chocolatiers and pastry chefs know what works: something catches your eye from under the glass, reminds you of your childhood, and blows a soft wind of nostalgia. Here is a small selection of confections I have discovered over the course of my visits.

Iranian Pistachio and Blackcurrant Marshmallow Square
Pain de Sucre

Blackcurrants on one hand, bits of pistachio on the other: these two flavors intermingle deliciously. The Orange Blossom is also exquisite, recalling notes of Haribo Chamallows, only more delicate and subtle. The chocolate and coconut marshmallow is like a big cube of chocolate mousse rolled in grated coconut. The portions are generous and the texture ultra-soft and melting. You also have to try the calissons, especially the chestnut honey flavor. They're a little crunchy from the almonds, which seem to be more roughly chopped here (which I like, because it gives it more 'chew' and more length on the palate), and are flavored heavily with candied orange.

Pain de Sucre? The pastries that emerge from the imagination of Nathalie Robert and Didier Mathray are certainly sublime, but so are their little morsels of confectionery! Personally, I have never managed to leave the shop without at least one marshmallow square. (See also page 36.)

Flower-flavored Marshmallow Squares
La Pâtisserie des Martyrs

Jasmine, orange blossom, or rose: these flowers are troublemakers. In the form of meltingly soft marshmallows, they are a mouthful of wonder. At the same time, they infuse the marshmallows with indulgent aromas with which you wouldn't mind perfuming your skin. The chocolate version makes you feel like you're eating an excellent chocolate mousse. I should add that these marshmallows are rather dense (and filling) and that one or two are enough. For the moment, anyway. In an hour, we'll be ready for more.

La Pâtisserie des Martyrs? Sébastien Gaudard opened his first shop with one idea in mind: to create a line of ultra-classic desserts. While they are more discreet than the pastries, these marshmallow squares are no less of a sugar rush. (See also pages 8 and 46.)

In the Mood for Sweets

These confections are not made to be eaten by the pound (unlike the candy I got at the bakery as a child). With their dense texture, their powerful aroma, and their naturally very present 'sucrosity', they are meant to be eaten in small bites so as to enjoy all of their nuances and benefits. After months of tasting sweets and smiling like a fool, I'm sure that sugar has an immediate effect on one's mood. I'd bet my life on it.

For addresses, see page 121.

1. Pain de Sucre

2. Iranian pistachio and blackcurrant marshmallows
   at Pain de Sucre

3. Chocolate and coconut marshmallows
   at Pain de Sucre

4. and 5. Inside La Pâtisserie des Martyrs

1. Caramels at Jacques Genin
2. Inside Jacques Genin
3. Fruit jellies at Jacques Genin
4. Kanougas at Pariès
5. Slices of touron at Pariès

♥ *Mango-Passion Caramel*
Jacques Genin

Generously portioned (it takes me several bites), with a sharp exotic fruit flavor and a texture that's got just the right amount of stickiness, this intensely tart caramel is a sensation. As for the nut-flavored caramels, the caramel base is salted just right and the nuts crunch deliciously under your teeth. Pistachio, almond, walnut, hazelnut, macadamia, pecan, or cashew — he makes them all! At the shop, they recommend keeping the caramels in the refrigerator and taking them out just seconds before eating. The cool sensation that results really does bring out the best in the caramel!

Jacques Genin? In Paris, his mango-passion caramel first made a name for itself in the luxury hotels and restaurants where it was served alongside coffee. But that was before Jacques Genin opened his own shop: how wonderful to be able to treat yourself a whole bagful! (See also pages 62 and 98.)

Kanougas
Pariès

These big, melt-in-your-mouth caramels come in several flavors. I confess to a weakness for the chocolate, with its nice cocoa color and very pronounced chocolate taste. The coffee flavor and the one filled with hazelnuts have the gift of reminding me of the first time I discovered caramel as a child. But I think they are even better than the ones I ate at the time, which were not from Pariès.

Pariès? Gâteau Basque, touron, chocolate: this century-old shop in Saint-Jean-de-Luz perfectly prepares all of the classic Basque sweets, but its oldest specialty is the Kanouga, a caramel variety created by the chocolatier Jacques Damestoy in 1905. (See also page 23.)

Fruit Jellies
Jacques Genin

Intense flavors in a small portion. The flavor combinations have been composed with delicacy and poetry: raspberry-rose, mango-passion, and so on. As for the simple flavors, they are not the ones we often see: banana, melon, mirabelle plum, etc. The texture of the jelly is firm and the taste of the fruit very present.

Jacques Genin? Always striving for perfection, Jacques Genin reveals the taste of fruit just as well as he does that of caramel or chocolate. The fruit is carefully chosen and the balance of sugar perfectly achieved. (See also pages 62 and 98.)

CBS
Henri Le Roux

CBS, as in caramel au beurre salé, or salted butter caramel. A perfect combination of soft and sticky, this caramel with very present notes of salt is one of the most indulgent and one of the most balanced — not to be missed in the world of caramel! The raspberry flavor has a bit of a crunch from the seeds of the fruit. The buckwheat variety, a pure product of Brittany, has a surprising taste. Then there is the Japanese-inspired yuzu matcha, which brings together green tea and notes of citrus. Mmmm, it's so good!

Henri Le Roux? The caramélier of Quiberon is the reason for the popularity of the salted butter caramel, thanks to his (trademarked) CBS, which was created in 1977 and has since won many awards. The shop still masters its subject well. (See also page 70.)

 Fruit Jellies
Henri Le Roux

A veritable homage to fruit. Whether it be peach, mandarin, or strawberry, the taste of the fruit is always incredibly well transcribed. Moreover, it makes me feel like I'm eating more of a pulp than a jelly (which is often too sweet for me). Another important detail, this fruit jelly is not rolled in sugar, which means that it doesn't have the crunch of other versions, and is a little less sugary. The surface ends up being slightly 'crusted', as if it were dried, and offers a little resistance under the teeth, which I adore.

Henri Le Roux? As it does for its caramels and chocolates, the shop works in the purest respect for its product. Authentic flavors, considered textures, careful presentations — this is the haute couture of the pâte de fruit. (See also page 70.)

Sweet Nostalgia

While I do like the new flavors that we find at different times of year (Christmas spices, strawberry or mint in the summer), I admit I am always seduced by caramels with timeless flavors like coffee, chocolate, or hazelnut, which, for me, are a direct path to childhood memories. Chewing on a coffee-flavored caramel always takes me back in time.

For addresses, see page 121.

1. Inside Henri Le Roux
2. and 4. Caramels at Henri Le Roux
3. Fruit jellies at Henri Le Roux

Frozen Desserts

The experience of intensely flavorful artisanal ice cream engenders a unique sensation. You feel like you're actually biting into the fruit, the vanilla, or the chocolate, purely through a recipe and the savoir-faire of its creator. It's no secret that to produce this result the artisan glacier must be as generous as possible with the quantity and quality of the ingredients. I would add that any season is a good season when you are lucky enough to have truly excellent ice cream.

♥ *Gianduja Ice Cream*
Pozzetto

Imagine the best chocolate spread in the world as an ice cream. With gianduja from Torino (a hazelnut chocolate paste that Italians go crazy for), you can taste the Piedmont hazelnuts, the dark chocolate, and the sweet indulgence. It is so rich in flavor, dense and opaque, that a few spoonfuls suffice. As for the Sicilian pistachio (without food coloring) and nougat flavors, both are literally nuts in ice cream form. The sorbets are exceptional: fig, kiwi, melon — they make you feel like you're eating the fruit itself!

Pozzetto? A 100% Italian artisanal label that has adapted to the French market by using French milk in its ice cream. On the sorbet side, the flavors available always reflect the fruit that is currently in season.

Frozen Yogurt
It Mylk

Served Italian-style in a spiral, this frozen yogurt is very refreshing because it is only lightly sweetened (with agave syrup). I particularly like the plain version, which foregrounds the milky and slightly tart sensation of the yogurt. But you can also choose strawberry or cocoa (which tastes like a frozen chocolate mousse) and cover it in toppings like bits of caramel, mini-macarons, cookies, strawberries, or mango. The skim yogurt used is made at the Ferme de Viltain, 17 kilometers outside Paris.

It Mylk? Having grown tired of the worlds of finance and marketing, sisters Mathilde and Constance Lorenzi decided to live their dream by creating their own company, inspired by the frozen yogurt that is all the rage across the Atlantic.

Top Quality Ice Cream

A good artisanal ice cream is ice cream that doesn't have too much water and air added to increase volume while lowering costs. Only the ingredients necessary to make the ice cream should enter into its composition (milk, eggs, cream, and flavors). This explains why it is so much denser than industrial ice cream and why it usually takes just a few spoonfuls to fill you up!

For addresses, see page 121.

1. Ice cream at Pozzetto
2. A salesperson at Pozzetto
3. An It Mylk stand
4. Frozen yogurt at It Mylk

1. A salesperson at Grom
2. Grom
3. Ice cream at Bac à Glaces
4. Inside Bac à Glaces
5. Inside Berthillon
6. Sorbet at Berthillon

Coffee Ice Cream
Grom

An espresso must have sneaked into this very strong coffee ice cream (from Slow-Food labeled beans produced on the Huehuetenango, a plateau in Guatemala, it says) for it to be so intense. The simultaneously creamy and whipped texture (which might seem contradictory, but not so here) gives it an unusual softness that slides happily onto your spoon. I also like the Crema di Grom, made from corn flour biscuits and dark chocolate, and the trans-alpine curiosities of the day, like the sheep's milk ricotta ice cream with caramelized almonds and sesame.

Grom? Behind the counter, the sales staff speak Italian, Japanese, French, and English (I overheard them all) — what polyglots! With shops in Italy, New York, Malibu, Tokyo and Osaka, this Torino-based company uses premium, environmentally conscious ingredients.

♥ Strawberry-Mint Sorbet
Bac à Glaces

'Fine Sorbets' says one of the wooden signs that cover the walls of the shop. That is exactly what you get when you taste this sorbet, with its flavor of perfectly ripe strawberries and a subtle hint of mint. Have we ever found a better pairing than that of mint and strawberry? I think not. Also not to be missed, the almond paste sorbet. Underneath its rich texture and subdued color, its strong yet refreshing almond flavor is unexpected. I should add that the tuile biscuit planted in the cup is a crunchy, delicious bonus.

Le Bac à Glaces? Nothing seems to change at this family-run shop, which has been on the rue du Bac for over thirty years. Each hour brings a different clientele. From a lunch among friends or colleagues (around a table full of tarts and galettes) to the parents and children who flock here after school, the tables are always full. Thankfully, they also sell ice cream to go, through a window opening onto the street.

♥ Vineyard Peach Sorbet
Berthillon

A sublime wine-red color, a very pronounced fruit flavor, and a lot of length on the palate: this sorbet transports you directly to the vineyards! The wild strawberry flavor, with its little pieces of fruit, is perfectly delicate; as for the blood orange, it brings out all of the nuances of the citrus. For die-hard fans of extra-dark chocolate, the cocoa sorbet is quite bold. Among the ice cream varieties, the nut flavors are chock full of their star ingredient. The praline and pine nut flavor, with pieces of pine nut, expresses itself differently in every spoonful, and the hazelnut brings out the flavor of the nut more faithfully than most of the ones I've tried.

Berthillon? Founded in 1954, it is undoubtedly the most famous ice cream shop in Paris. The length of the line outside varies from day to day, but you always have to wait. I should mention that the little salon next to the shop is cozy and very elegant; ice cream eaten there must have just a little more soul. Obviously, it is hard to get a spot.

For addresses, see page 121.

Mirabelle Plum Sorbet
Mister Ice

All of the delicacy of this little Lorraine plum, whose season is so short, is revealed in this sorbet. A supple texture, with not much sugar and a good fruit flavor, is all it takes. The pistachio ice cream, with its bits of pistachio that crunch under your teeth and amplify the flavor, is also delicious. I glanced at the coffee soufflé just before leaving and now I dream of going back to try it.

Mister Ice? Fabien Foenix, who provides ice cream for many professional establishments, has his own little shop in a forgotten corner of the 17th arrondissement. The charming salesperson is not stingy with the little spoons and will let you taste all the flavors you like. I should add, however, that a few modern touches wouldn't hurt the decor.

 ## Vanilla Ice Cream
À la Mère de Famille

I don't know how many beans slide into this cream as it is being prepared, but whenever I see it, the abundance of vanilla seeds per square inch always surprises me. With its intense vanilla flavor, as you can imagine, its rather pronounced egg cream flavor, and its perfectly creamy texture, it's one of my favorites! You must also taste the milky, tart fromage blanc and morello cherry ice cream, which can become addictive. Not to mention the quite sophisticated vacherins that leave their delectable mark on dessert.

À la Mère de Famille? While the variety of chocolate bonbons doesn't change much throughout the year, Chef Julien Merceron can be quite daring when it comes to ice cream, and to new frozen creations in particular, like the frozen vanilla-praline tart, which I will surely never forget. (See also page 69.)

Cup or Cone?

In a shop that sells ice cream to go, when faced with the question of 'cup or cone?', I always take the cup. To be honest, I worry that the wafer or the waffle of the cone may be of inferior quality, and would prefer to end my tasting experience with the sensation of the ice cream rather than that of a soggy biscuit.

For addresses, see page 121.

1. Inside À la Mère de Famille
2. Ice cream at À la Mère de Famille
3. The original À la Mère de Famille

1. Ice cream at Raimo
2. Inside Raimo
3. Inside La Tropicale
4. Ice cream at La Tropicale
5. Ice cream at Martine Lambert
6. The ice cream stand at Martine Lambert

Three-Spice Ice Cream
Raimo

Strange and captivating, this ice cream flavored with cardamom, coriander, and black pepper leaves the texture of the spices on your tongue, along with a pleasant heat (I know, this seems contradictory to the nature of ice cream). Refreshing in the summer, the lemon-basil sorbet stands out with the tartness of the lemon and the freshness of the basil, which linger nicely on the palate. I love to pair it with a fromage blanc sorbet, which adds a hint of unctuousness and a milky flavor.

Raimo? One of the oldest and best ice cream shops in Paris, originally located on the boulevard de Reuilly in the 12th arrondissement. The space also houses a pleasant tea salon. Two branches have opened in neighborhoods with more pedestrian traffic.

Bissap Ginger Sorbet
La Tropicale

Take the tart notes of a hibiscus flower and a ginger root that lingers on the palate, infuse together and freeze, and you have this highly refreshing sorbet. The soy milk matcha (Japanese green tea) sorbet is another pleasant curiosity, not to mention the beet-blackcurrant and the bell pepper-orange-espelette pepper sorbets. The date-walnut and orange blossom-pistachio ice cream varieties also look very good.

La Tropicale? A little neighborhood tea salon with a relaxed atmosphere, which had the wonderful idea of making its own ice cream and focusing on unexpected flavors.

For addresses, see page 121.

Caramel Ice Cream
Martine Lambert

When cooked in a copper pot, caramel is bound to be intensely flavored, and in this ice cream made from rich Normandy milk, it all makes sense. The Martinique flavor, made with vanilla, orange, rum, and candied orange peel, is a little slice of heaven that makes me want to learn to speak Creole. On the sorbet side, blood orange, grapefruit, candied ginger and Périgord raspberry are just some of the temptations you should give in to.

Martine Lambert? Having spent her childhood vacations in Deauville, she returned there in the 1970s to build her reputation as an artisan glacier. Today, her ice cream brings joy to Deauville and Paris, maintaining the same high standards: using only premium, high quality basic ingredients and letting nothing get in the way of their natural flavor.

Pastry Chefs, Too!

Many pastry chefs are moving into ice cream (Sébastien Gaudard, Pierre Hermé, Philippe Conticini, Hugo & Victor, and many others). But it is hard to select the best among all of the new creations that are sometimes only available in the summer, or for a particular event. I'll leave it to you to discover their offerings as you visit each of their shops.

Where to Eat

Choosing from among the desserts in a display or on
a cart, enjoying a calm, luxurious atmosphere, chatting
for hours on end — I love these special moments that
you can only have in a tea salon. For reasons of space
or cost, many pastry chefs have to limit their shops to
takeout sales. Pretty tea salons are becoming rare and
that's what makes them all the more sought after. Whether
at a chocolate bar, a Japanese counter, a timeless luxury
hotel, or a cross between any of the above, the moment
should be unique, peaceful, and indulgent.

♥ *Colorova*

It means 'multicolored' in Polish. A shop, a place to eat (I love its pop art colors, its exotic style, and the comfortable furniture), and a laboratory (cakes are made there all day long, so as you can imagine, the aromas of melting chocolate and pie crust browning in the oven are not exactly rare), Colorova puts us at the heart of the matter. Behind this hybrid storefront, the pastry chef Guillaume Gil and his fiancée, Charlotte Siles, have thought of everything. Their pastries are distinguished by a sense of balance and elegance; flavors are in keeping with current fashion and make it hard to choose. While the sesame-yuzu caramel seems to be calling me, I opt for the matcha green tea and pink grapefruit cheesecake. On its sablé base, the layers of cream and ganache are full of green tea and the little slices of grapefruit add a fresh, bitter note. Worth noting: there are also delicate and flavorful savory items served at lunch or brunch (reserve as far in advance as possible).

Acide Salon de Thé

An air of modernity blows through this space opened in early 2013 by the pastry chef Jonathan Blot, creator of the Acide Macaron shop a few doors down. From the entrance, the display of classic pastries (religieuses, tarts, cheesecake), cookies, and viennoiseries whets your appetite. The long, narrow room leads to the laboratory where we can hear voices, the sounds of molding and kneading. I love this dynamic that blends in with the experience of eating. The lights are soft, like the blond tones of the tables and the parquet, contrasting with the midnight blue wall behind the counter: a perfect balance. The Gariguette strawberry tart has the last word. The crust breaks apart loudly, but the fruit is devilishly flavorful and the thin layer of vanilla cream softly absorbs the shock. Perfect accompanied by herbal tea with floral notes (hibiscus, rose hip and orange peels, apple slices, marigolds). I also love the attention paid to the china: a beautiful tea service and plates decorated with dark blue and gold crossbars.

Jacques Genin

While the chocolates and pastries are made upstairs, on the ground floor you'll find the shop and the tea salon. Stone walls, thick, red velvet wall coverings like at the theater, armchairs that are comfortable without being slouchy, and an immense spiral staircase leading up to the laboratory: there is nothing ordinary about the decor. Jacques Genin's mille-feuille is among the best in Paris and draws a crowd that lines up at the entrance to the tea salon, especially on the weekend. During the week, it's much calmer. A mille-feuille made to order makes all the difference, taking you to extremes of crunchiness and freshness. One stroke of the fork and knife and the cream spills out at the sides, the crispiness of the layers will have you in tears, and the rich, fresh cream reveals a nicely balanced caramel flavor (I chose caramel, but there are also vanilla and chocolate). With a particularly good café crème, this is nirvana. And then there's the little plate of bonbons placed delicately on the table, prolonging the experience and the discovery of Jacques Genin's talents. (See also pages 62 and 83.)

For addresses, see page 121.

1. Raspberry tart at Colorova
2. and 3. Inside Colorova
4. Acide Salon de thé
5. Marshmallows at Jacques Genin
6. Inside Jacques Genin

1. A salesperson fills creampuffs at La Maison du Chou
2. La Maison du Chou
3. Chocolates at Jean-Paul Hévin
4. The Guayaquil at Jean-Paul Hévin
5. The Saint-Honoré at Carette
6. Inside one of the Carette locations

♥ *La Maison du Chou*

In the Saint-Germain-des-Prés neighborhood, on the place de Furstenberg (one of the most charming squares in Paris, if you ask me), across from the Delacroix Museum, you might hardly notice La Maison du Chou. This shop founded in 2013 by the Michelin-starred chef Manuel Martinez (of Le Relais Louis XIII) plays marvelously with the creation of an 'old-fashioned' ambience around a classic pastry. Walk into the miniscule tea salon with its white walls, its old, dark wood furniture, and its three tables (packed on the weekends), and look. Time seems to have stood still. The menu is stuffed with other things, but really, there's only the cream puff, a delicate and delicious chou filled with a light cream made from eggs, sugar, and fromage blanc, which makes it very contemporary. There are three flavors: plain, coffee, and chocolate. I have a certain preference for the plain, which is extremely refreshing with its tart flavor of fromage blanc.

Jean-Paul Hévin Chocolate Bar

On the upper floor of his shop on the rue Saint-Honoré, this salon is one of the rare food establishments in Paris dedicated entirely to chocolate. The menu of hot and iced chocolate is lengthy, and some of the preparations turn out to be quite daring; I'm thinking of the matcha-chocolate, the raspberry-chocolate, and especially the oyster-chocolate. I prefer to stick with the classics and order a Colombian cocoa hot chocolate. Fluid, not too thick, and not at all sweetened (or at least, that's the impression it gives), it's a chocolatey enchantment that leaves a trace on your lips. Ideally? Wait until it cools down a bit to able to smell all of the aromas and enjoy all of its creaminess. JPH's pastries are also available, like the Guayaquil (almond-cocoa cake with very cocoa-y, almost bitter chocolate mousse — a pure chocolate experience) or the excellent chocolate tart. In my opinion, hot chocolate and chocolate pastries don't go together. I've tried it and I find that the aromas of each collide with one another and create confusion. (See also page 64.)

Carette Place des Vosges

This institution on the place du Trocadéro has opened up a second shop in the Marais. The atmosphere is one of an old-style tea salon where things are a bit rushed. The stone and cream-colored decor are in keeping with that of the arcades of the place des Vosges. When you are sitting in the little room in the back, you can see the mirrors reflecting the pretty flowered courtyard behind the windows. Personally, I recommend that you stay with the classics (I was less impressed by the 'revisited' Mont-Blanc and the Paris-Carette), with, notably, the Opéra. It is heavy on the coffee, I should warn you, and highly saturated, which is nice, because the coffee adds a kick and the 'wetness' makes it quite moist (I don't like it as much when it's dry). The other nice surprise here is the Saint-Honoré. The cream puffs are delicate, the caramel very fine, the vanilla whipped cream rather dense, as is the pastry cream hidden in the choux, and the puff pastry base has just the right amount of butter. In sum, a classic done right.

For addresses, see page 121.

♥ *La Pâtisserie des Rêves*

After setting your sights on one of the cake-filled glass domes, head to the back of the shop to discover the tea salon. Looking out onto a group of courtyards and gardens, the calm, sunny terrace is ideal. If the weather isn't nice enough to sit outside and you are in a hurry for your dessert, the inside is a pleasant, white, light-filled space. I should add that Wednesday is kids' day. If you have a craving for a classic, I recommend the Saint-Honoré. On a perfect puff pastry base, the vanilla whipped cream and generous, caramel-covered choux seem to be thoroughly enjoying themselves. Another excellent choice is the Paris-Brest, whose extra dose of praline will turn even the most die-hard fans pale. Personally, I confess to a weakness for the chef's creations. The Calisson, Dragée and Pur Vanille entremets reach staggering heights of flavor. (See also page 27.)

Helmut Newcake

How gratifying for the gluten intolerant! All of the classics (éclair, religieuse, tarts) and a few creations are represented in this shop-tea salon without losing an ounce of richness. Its founders — Marie Tagliaferro, a gluten-intolerant pastry chef, and her husband — have created a space with a relaxed atmosphere and a simple, inviting decor that blends perfectly into the neighborhood surrounding the Canal Saint-Martin. There are a few tables lined up along the pastry case, but I prefer the little room in the back with a glass roof that lights up the dishes. With its golden yellow cream and the fruit that I can never resist, the passion fruit-hazelnut tart is ordered within seconds. The rather tart passion fruit cream is balanced by a thin layer of hazelnut paste and a crunchy pie crust — I'm in heaven. In a pretty, retro tea service, the purple color and acidic notes of the herbal tea, an infusion of hibiscus, nettle, and aloe vera, are absolutely delightful.

1 J. Rue Scribe

This elegant teahouse is connected to the Hotel Scribe next door. Because there are so few tables, you are sure to be able to enjoy its enchanting decor in peace: a sublime chandelier, Corinthian columns, big couches, a discreet sense of chic, and exquisitely kind service. You will not be in a hurry to leave. For even more privacy, take the jet black spiral staircase up to the library-like mezzanine. Among the chef's creations, I choose the one made of panna cotta, white chocolate, and yuzu, which offers nice textural contrasts (creamy and crunchy) and very tart, milky flavors. The chef doesn't hold back on the acidity of the yuzu — it's bold and will make you blink. Among the vertiginous selection of teas (from India, China, Japan), the white tea from Fujian province, China, known as 'Silver Needle', is a beverage of the utmost delicacy.

For addresses, see page 121.

1. The *Paris-Brest* at La Pâtisserie des Rêves
2. The lemon tart and the Saint-Honoré
   at La Pâtisserie des Rêves
3. Inside 1T. Rue Scribe
4. The display case at Helmut Newcake
5. Pastry chef Jean-Baptiste Aybran
   of 1T. Rue Scribe

1. The Toraya tea salon
2. A pastry at the Toraya tea salon
3. A box of *wagashi* at Toraya
4. The Walaku tea salon
5. A pastry at the Walaku tea salon

Exotic Flavors: A Special Section

Sometimes pastry shops can make you feel as if you're traveling and visiting other cultures. Sit down at a counter to watch Japanese crêpes brown, place an order at an American-style cake shop, or have an Austrian cake as the cuckoo clock chirps. It's all possible. In Paris.

★ Japan in Paris

Toraya

A fixture in Japan for over 500 years, this traditional pastry shop opened a branch in Paris about 30 years ago. Its elegant, intimate, and very comfortable tea salon is quite popular with those in the know. Still, there's always a first time and I'm sure that once you've had yours, you'll quickly develop a taste for the shop's specialty: wagashi, pastries made of a mix of rice and wheat flours, red beans, and agar-agar, whose seasonal shapes are veritable sculptures. On the menu, each wagashi is presented in a very poetic fashion: 'A pearly-white cake, whose sensual forms are drawn out at each end to create a beak and a tail, the Uzura Yaki has the streamlined contours of a little quail. Its feathers are represented by a simple pressed stroke and stamped with a hot iron. This cake, whose name has been recognized since before the Edo era (1603-1868), is made of a fine gyûhi rice paste and filled with sesame-flavored azuki red bean paste.' This is the one I chose. It has an elastic, resistant dough, filled with a sweet puree of red beans that is reminiscent of chestnut. Accompanied by a cup of matcha for its 'kick' of bitterness and green, it transports you to Japan in your mind.

♥ Walaku

This miniscule tea salon founded by the owner of Aida (a delicate Japanese restaurant in the 7th arrondissement) is an enchantment. The wooden screen that separates the tables while allowing light to pass and eyes to see through, the little curtains (you know, the ones that come just down to your neck), the sophistication of the china and the tea service, the eight seats that encourage calm and discretion — Japan sneaks into every detail. One of the specialties of the house is dorayaki (a kind of super soft honey pancake), which is cooked in front of you (if you sit at the counter) and filled with seasonal ingredients. In the summer, this could mean sweet, melting red beans (azuki), whipped cream, and a few pieces of fresh strawberry, accompanied by a cup of sencha (green tea) or hojicha (roasted tea). For connoisseurs, there is also a selection of wagashi (traditional Japanese pastries). Note: Walaku also has a really nice prix fixe lunch menu.

For addresses, see page 121.

Ciel

Opened by Youlin Ly, the man behind the famous Sola and Saké Bar restaurants (5th arrondissement), this space is hypnotizing in its brightness from the moment you walk in the door. The light shade of soft wood that covers the counter, the immaculately white tea service and dessert boxes (with an incredible pleat on top), all make you feel like you're floating on cotton. Ciel serves one, and only one, kind of pastry: angel food cake, as Americans call it. Today, it comes in matcha, yuzu, pink praline, and vanilla-caramel flavors, among others, in individual portions (there are also larger sizes for groups). I choose the matcha accompanied by a matcha-yuzu iced tea from the excellent shop Jugetsudo (6th arrondissement). Stamped with the name of the shop, this pretty green, airy cake (it reminds you of a sponge) hides a delicious matcha cream center. Without much sugar, the matcha flavor is highlighted and is exquisitely light.

★ American Delights

She's Cake

A clever name for this little storefront dedicated entirely to cheesecake. Savory (goat cheese, honey and walnuts, or comté cheese and mushrooms, to mention only two) or sweet (cappuccino, caramel-pecan, seasonal fruits), this American dessert is the perfect medium for Séphora Saada's creativity. Behind the display case filled with cheesecakes, each more alluring than the next, and a few tables, you can glimpse the laboratory and the pastry chef with her chef's hat on, hard at work. We are clearly at the heart of the matter. The refrigerated case is a little noisy, but the cheesecake itself will make you forget all about it. Round and visually seductive, its cream is particularly dense, with a slight taste of petit-suisse cheese and a speculoos-flavored crust that could use just a little more crunch.

♥ Sugarplum Cake Shop

In this American-style coffee shop, the cakes are surrounded by tough competition: gigantic cookies, a pecan pie with an appetizing fall color, Rice Krispie Treats (big cubes of puffed rice and marshmallows), or peanut butter cornflakes — I don't know where to look! Here everything proceeds American-style: you order at the counter, pay, and sit down. Walls with stone peeking through, tables scattered here and there — the decor is simple and comfortable. And you should know that the terrace is sunny in the afternoon. After ten long minutes of hemming and hawing, I go for the carrot cake, which must be 5 inches tall, alternating layers of carrot-cinnamon cake with a dense cream-cheese icing. With a delicious iced tea, it turns out to be rather light, and impossible to stop eating. Worth noting, the (American) founders have their laboratory in the back and make incredible cakes to order.

For addresses, see page 121.

1. Inside Ciel
2. Pastry chef Séphora Saada of She's Cake
3. Inside the Sugarplum Cake Shop

1. Pastelaria Belém
2. The display case at Pastelaria Belém
3. The window display at Kaffeehaus
4. Inside Kaffeehaus

★ Lisbon within Reach

Pastelaria Belem

Inspired by the Pastéis de Belém pastry shop in Lisbon, which has been making pastéis for over 200 years, this Parisian shop is rich in color and authenticity. From the azulejos (typical Portuguese white and blue ceramics) that decorate the walls to the slightly antiquated model boats, to the counter where people of every generation rub elbows as they sip their coffee, you'll feel like you're in the heart of Lisbon. Bend your ear: it's likely you'll hear only Portuguese. If you've never been, but dream of traveling to Lisbon, get yourself to the rue Boursault (17th arrondissement)! The pastel de nata is divine. Heavy and generous, it offers the kind of contrast that we like in the pastel: a very thin crust, layered and crispy, and a thick layer of nicely sweetened egg cream. My god, it's good!

★ Eastward Ho!

Kaffeehaus

Here, the pastry chef Ralf Edeler celebrates the sweets of Germany and Eastern Europe. A Black Forest hidden under piles of chocolate shavings and whipped cream, a Sachertorte with an extra-generous amount of chocolate, fromage blanc cakes, and pies overflowing with fruit: the display case is an enchantment for the eyes. And I haven't even mentioned the cookies and kouglofs displayed all around the shop. In short, it is a generous place. In the upstairs tea salon, the warm wood, the paper place mats on the tables, the little collection of cuckoo clocks (one of which chirps every hour), and the vases of flowers evoke the atmosphere of an Austrian chalet. With its thin, golden crust and unadorned fruit, the apple strudel is simple and delicious. A little jar of unsweetened whipped cream is served alongside, which is very much appreciated for the refreshing sensation of the cream. Note that the tea salon also doubles as a restaurant at lunchtime, continuing its focus on Eastern European specialties.

For addresses, see page 121.

What a Palace!

The grand palaces or luxury hotels of Paris often propose a nice menu of sweets at teatime. Prices follow accordingly, I should stress: figure about 30 euros for a pastry and tea, 45 euros for a full 'teatime' service. But how lovely to pamper oneself for an afternoon in the luxury and comfort of a palace!

Plaza Athénée

At the Plaza Hotel, avenue Montaigne, teatime takes place in the Galerie des Gobelins. Perhaps not the most intimate setting, since clients are seated facing each other along each side of the gallery (no better spot for people watching). But if you like to bathe in an atmosphere of supreme luxury, the comfort of the seats, the giant chandeliers, the cream-colored decor and the wafting sounds of a harp create the perfect illusion for the time it takes to sit for a snack. The dessert cart by chefs Christophe Michalak and Jean-Marie Hiblot makes its entrance. The mille-feuille 'by the meter' (that is, in an extra-large portion), one of the best sellers, stands out immediately. Laid on its side, it seems like it's lying down. The maître-d' slices into it carefully. It's sublime, with an indecently thick layer of cream on top, which is slightly foamy and not too sweet, giving depth to the vanilla, and very crunchy and rather well-browned layers of puff pastry (I think this is a conscious choice by the pastry chef, one that gives it a lot of flavor). Surely one of the best mille-feuilles I've tasted. In season, the strawberry tart is another sweet temptation.

 Shangri-La

The first European branch of a Hong Kong-based group, the Shangri-La has taken over the former residence of Prince Roland Bonaparte (16th arrondissement). Two options are available for teatime (from 3 to 6 p.m.): the cozy salons of the lounge, all in upholstered wood, with wide, chic armchairs, chandeliers, touches of gold, and fireplaces that work in the winter; and the restaurant La Bauhinia, which has a more Asian feel, with its sublime skylights, its celadon green colors, its orchids, and, as always, very comfortable seating. At teatime, particular care is given to the setting of the tablecloth, the perfectly aligned silverware, and the three-tiered serving platter. We'll start with the savory sandwiches made of different kinds of sliced bread and fillings. There is also the tier of small cakes (canelé, financier, a jar of gianduja) and that of the mini-pastries (lemon tart, Opéra, cream puffs, chocolate entremets). Not to mention the warm scones served on the side with whipped cream. Everything is very sophisticated and perfectly executed by the pastry chef François Perret.

For addresses, see page 121.

1. The lychee-raspberry entremets at Shangri-La
2. Pastry Chef François Perret of Shangri-La
3. The La Bauhinia tea salon at Shangri-La
4. The *bûche de Noël* at Shangri-La

1. Brunch at the Royal Monceau
2. Pastry chef Yann Couvreur of Prince de Galles
3. Les Heures bar at Prince de Galles

Le Royal Monceau

In this luxury hotel that is both contemporary in style (designed by Philippe Starck) and devilishly comfortable (I would stay there for breakfast and dinner and overnight if I could), Pierre Hermé supervises all of the desserts. When I think about it, it's the only place I know where you can order and eat the pastries of the master: none of his other establishments has a tea salon. At 3 p.m., we take our place in one of the hidden corners of Le Bar Long (there are several bars) or at one of the center tables to observe (or be seen by) the hotel's artistic and touristic fauna. The tiered platter arrives. The finger sandwiches are rather (not to say very) classic, while the scones — cocoa and Ispahan (Pierre Hermé's famous combination of raspberry, rose, and lychee) — are quite surprising. With double cream, they're even better. The Ispahan, the miniature cheesecake, and the coffee macaron add a sublime final note. And I mustn't forget the hot chocolate, prepared from chocolate and water — a delight.

Prince de Galles

Ever since the renovation of this hotel on the avenue George V, its Art Deco style persists, but in a more contemporary and intimate relation with its clients. Teatime takes place at the bar or on the patio, from 3 to 6 p.m. At this time of day, I like to stay inside, in the comfort of a salon; the cozy, luminous bar is ideal. It is designed around a clock theme (the bar is called Les Heures), and the cart and platter arrive in unusual round shapes. Oolong tea, finger sandwiches, eggs mimosa, crab wrap, avocado and curry mayonnaise, and a mini-bagel with salmon to start — I'm in heaven. The marble cake covered in fine chocolate and the hazelnut cake are divine. The tart of the day — fig and shiso (an herb with a mentholated flavor) — is surprising and very delicate. Not to mention the well-caramelized kouign amann, the kouglof, cookies, and small chocolate cakes that reflect the attention the pastry chef Yann Couvreur brings to each of the elements that comprise this sweet time of day.

Luxury Hotels: Intimidating?

I tend to agree: the monumental doors, the 'bonjour' from the concierge, or the looks from other clients can sometimes make walking into a luxury hotel an intimidating experience. But once you're comfortably seated in one of those big armchairs, being served by a staff determined to meet your every need, you'll quickly forget. You're inside? Then relax and enjoy every moment!

For addresses, see page 121.

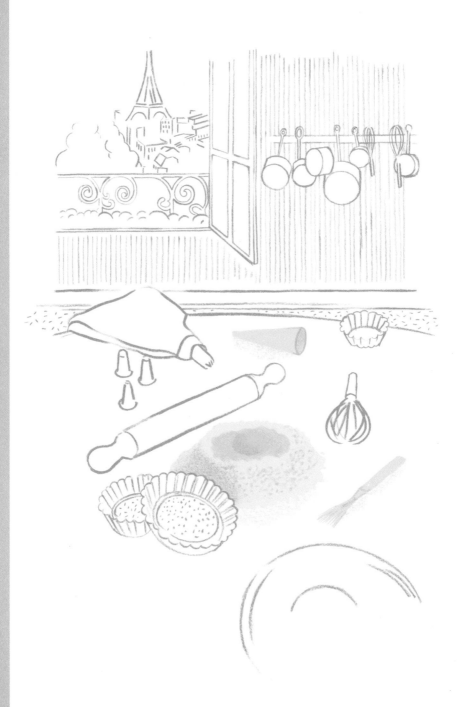

Where to Learn

While it's nice to let oneself go in the best pastry shops in Paris, sometimes you feel like creating your own confections. Here are a few places where you can get the best books on the subject or learn alongside qualified professionals in enjoyable settings, which doesn't hurt. Given their success, the historic cooking workshops have also started working in pastry, and famous Parisian chefs are opening their own schools, to the utmost delight of their admirers.

Librairie Gourmande

It's THE specialist bookstore in Paris. The pastry section is upstairs: books by pastry chefs, old, re-issued recipe books, trendy themes, and indispensable works for learning the basics (techniques from A to Z). They have it all! The owner, Deborah Dupont, knows just about everything there is to know about pastries in Paris, books in progress, shops about to open, and chefs to discover (it's not at all rare, by the way, to run into chefs who are there to stock their shelves). To stay informed about book signings by great pastry (and other) chefs, you must subscribe to her newsletter.

L'École de Cuisine Alain Ducasse

All of the spirit of Chef Alain Ducasse in a school means rigor, seriousness, and shiny kitchens to work in (with prices slightly higher than elsewhere). Lasting half a day, the 'Grande pâtisserie' class is very tempting: there you will learn how to prepare the desserts served in Alain Ducasse's three-star restaurants, such as grapefruit soufflé and baba au rhum. Four-hour classes on pastry basics are also offered, usually focusing on a few specific desserts, like kouign-amann, gâteau Basque, and chocolate-pear charlotte. If you want something more relaxed, there is a two-hour class called 'L'Instant pâtisserie', focusing on a theme ingredient, like chocolate, strawberry, or chestnut. Worth noting is M. Ducasse's incredible collection of mortars, displayed in the hallways of the school.

Michalak Master Class

Leave it to the intrepid and talented pastry chef Christophe Michalak (see also page 110) to create a school in his image — that is, dynamic and gourmand. Christophe Michalak teaches a few classes, but above all knows how to surround himself with very good pastry chefs. Spend two hours learning how to work with a key product like chocolate, praline, or caramel, or attend a three-hour demonstration-type workshop to learn how to create a traditional dessert or a chef's signature dessert — these were the options available at the recent opening of the school in late September 2013. Christophe Michalak doesn't just let his students leave: it's hard to resist the Atomic Cookies, Klakettes (chocolate and nuts), K7 Vidéo (filled with hazelnut and peanut praline), and other chocolate products in the 'take away' corner.

L'Atelier des Chefs

Well-established formulas, accessible chefs, and a modern touch: L'Atelier des Chefs has made itself indispensable in the world of cooking classes, and more and more in the realm of pastries! Basic techniques, macarons, American desserts, seasonal fruits, all chocolate or all caramel themes: the classes, lasting one and a half or two hours, aim for efficiency and some are organized for parents and their children to learn together. In most of the workshops, there is also a little shop that sells ingredients, books, and utensils. There are now seven Atelier des Chefs workshops in Paris — and counting.

For addresses, see page 121.

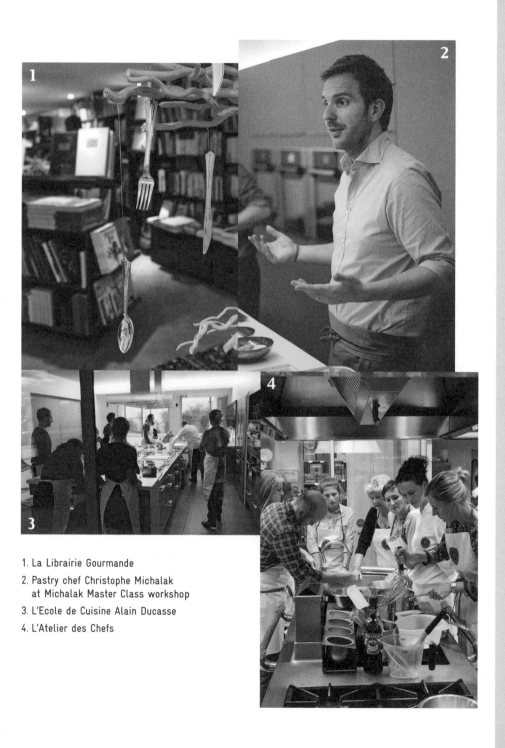

1. La Librairie Gourmande
2. Pastry chef Christophe Michalak
   at Michalak Master Class workshop
3. L'Ecole de Cuisine Alain Ducasse
4. L'Atelier des Chefs

1. L'Atelier des Sens
2. Cuisine Attitude Cyril Lignac
3. Chez Bogato
4. ChocoLatitudes

L'Atelier des Sens

Classes that ceaselessly adapt to new ideas and trends, good humor, convivial settings: L'Atelier des Sens has become a staple in Paris. Other than cooking, oenology, and cosmetics classes, it offers pastry classes in one-, two-, or three-hour formats. Floral flavors, ice cream and sorbet, childhood sweets, choux pastry, designer cakes, viennoiseries: you have a choice of original or more traditional themes. Classes for children (6 to 11 years old) are also offered. L'Atelier des Sens now has three branches in Paris.

Cuisine Attitude, Cyril Lignac

Looking out onto a pretty, hidden courtyard in the 3rd arrondissement, the workshop is well appointed and boasts a resolutely contemporary decor. Under its immense glass roof, a three-hour course zooms quickly by. With 'Choux pastry and its sweet variations,' 'Mille-feuilles', or 'Macarons', the classic themes answer all the questions you ask yourself when faced with these monuments of French pastry. The classes called 'Addicted to caramel' (like me), 'Addicted to soufflés', and 'Addicted to Strawberries' naturally target the monomaniacal among us. But there's something for everyone. I should add that the dates are announced well in advance but quickly fill up.

Chez Bogato

This concept, unique in Paris, was created by Anaïs Olmer, a young woman who went from advertising to cake creation. Full of sweet decorations, childhood candies, and fantastical cakes and cookies, the shop feels like something out of Hansel and Gretel. The workshops take place in the back, in the laboratory where the cookies in the shop and one-of-a-kind creations are made to order. 'Halloween', 'Rainbow Cookies', 'Little Squirrel Cookies', 'Monster Cookies': the workshops for children (on Wednesday, and all week during school vacations) have a sense of humor. Rest assured, adults have their own courses with themes revolving around the 'Great Classics' or 'Chez Bogato's Essentials', with new trends to follow. (See also page 36.)

ChocoLatitudes

Laurence Alemanno used to be a biologist; in particular, she studied cacao trees in producer countries. One day, she decided that she wanted to transmit all that she had discovered about cacao: its diversity, the importance of organic agriculture and fair trade, and the pleasure. On rue Daguerre in Paris, she opened a shop that is both a store and a place for tasting chocolates. The shop is kept cool (to better conserve the chocolate), but the hot chocolate that she makes every day is thick and varies according to the batches of chocolate that she wants to cook with. On Sunday, she runs tasting classes for those who want to learn everything there is to know about chocolate while developing a true taster's palate. (See also page 61.)

For addresses, see page 121.

Addresses
Alphabetical Listing

Note: Here you'll find addresses for all of the shops in Paris and the Île-de-France cited in this guide. If a shop is based in another part of France or in Belgium, the address of the original shop is also given. I have indicated the days each shop was closed at the time of printing. On Sunday, it's best to call to confirm that a shop will be open in the afternoon, since many boutiques close at 1 or 2 p.m., depending on the neighborhood. It is also possible that some shops will have closed permanently between the preparation and the publication of this guide, while many others will probably have opened.

A

Acide Salon de thé page 98
• 24, rue des Moines, 17ᵉ
09 83 87 05 09, closed Monday
www.acidemacaron.com

Aki Boulangerie page 41
• 16, rue Sainte-Anne, 1ᵉʳ
01 40 15 63 38, closed Sunday

À la Mère de Famille pages 69 and 92
• 82, rue Montorgueil, 2ᵉ, 01 53 40 82 78
• 70, rue Bonaparte, 6ᵉ
(not yet open at time of printing)
• 39, rue du Cherche-Midi, 6ᵉ,
01 42 22 49 99, closed Sunday
• 47, rue Cler, 7ᵉ,
01 45 55 29 74, closed Monday
• 33 and 35, rue du Faubourg-Montmartre,
9ᵉ, 01 47 70 83 69
• Printemps Haussmann,
64, boulevard Haussmann, 9ᵉ,
01 42 82 49 56, closed Sunday
• 59, rue de la Pompe, 16ᵉ, 01 45 04 73 19
• 107, rue Jouffroy-d'Abbans, 17ᵉ,
01 47 63 15 15, closed Sunday
• 30, rue Legendre, 17ᵉ, 01 47 63 52 94
• 7, avenue Charles-de-Gaulle,
94100 Saint-Maur, 01 42 83 81 49
www.lameredefamille.com

Arnaud Larher pages 36 and 64
• 93, rue de Seine, 6ᵉ,
01 43 29 38 15, closed Monday
• 53, rue Caulaincourt, 18ᵉ,
01 42 57 68 08, closed Monday
• 57, rue Damrémont, 18ᵉ,
01 42 55 57 97, closed Monday
www.arnaud-larher.com

Aux Merveilleux de Fred page 20
• 2, rue Monge, 5ᵉ,
01 43 54 63 72, closed Monday
• 94, rue Saint-Dominique, 7ᵉ,
01 47 53 91 34, closed Monday
• 129 bis, rue Saint-Charles, 15ᵉ,
01 45 79 72 47, closed Monday
• 29, rue de l'Annonciation, 16ᵉ,
01 45 20 13 82, closed Monday
• 7, rue de Tocqueville, 17ᵉ,
01 42 27 86 63, closed Monday
Lille
• Café Méo, 5-7, Grand'Place,
06 73 88 60 10, closed Monday
• 67, rue de la Monnaie,
03 20 51 99 59, closed Monday
• 336, rue Léon-Gambetta,
03 20 57 25 58
www.auxmerveilleux.com

B

Baillardran page 23
• 12, boulevard des Capucines, 9ᵉ,
01 47 42 39 88, closed Sunday
• Gare Montparnasse,
Bâtiment Voyageur, Level C, in front of
Track 13, 14ᵉ, 01 40 47 99 24
• Orly Airport, Terminal Ouest, Departure
Level, 94310 Orly, 01 49 75 53 04
Bordeaux
• Galerie des Grands-Hommes,
05 56 79 05 89, closed Sunday
• Centre commercial Auchan Bordeaux-Lac,
05 56 43 29 38
• Centre commercial Mériadeck,
05 56 24 68 40
• Gare Bordeaux Saint-Jean,
Departure Hall, Levels 0 and –1,
• 55, cours de l'Intendance,
05 56 52 92 64
• 41, rue des 3-Conils,
05 56 44 10 61
• 29, rue Porte-Dijeaux,
05 56 52 87 45
• 111, rue Porte-Dijeaux,
05 56 51 02 09
www.baillardran.com

Benoît Chocolats page 76
• 75, rue Saint-Antoine, 4ᵉ, 01 49 96 52 02,
closed Sunday
Angers
• 1, rue des Lices, 02 41 88 94 52,
closed Sunday and Monday
www.chocolats-benoit.com

Berthillon page 91
• 31, rue Saint-Louis-en-l'Île, 4ᵉ,
01 43 54 31 61, closed Monday and Tuesday
www.berthillon.fr

Blé Sucré page 35
• 7, rue Antoine-Vollon, 12ᵉ, 01 43 40 77 73,
closed Monday
www.blesucre.fr

Bread & Roses page 24
• 62, rue Madame, 6ᵉ, 01 42 22 06 06,
closed Sunday
• 25, rue Boissy-d'Anglas, 8ᵉ,
01 47 42 40 00, closed Sunday
www.breadandroses.fr

C

Café Pouchkine page 31
• 2, rue des Francs-Bourgeois, 3ᵉ,
01 42 72 97 05, open 7/7
• Printemps de la mode,
64, boulevard Haussmann, 9ᵉ,
01 42 82 43 31, closed Sunday
www.cafe-pouchkine.fr

Carette page 101
• 25, place des Vosges, 3ᵉ, 01 48 87 94 07
• 4, place du Trocadéro, 16ᵉ, 01 47 27 98 85
www.carette-paris.com

Carl Marletti page 8
• 51, rue Censier, 5ᵉ,
01 43 31 68 12, closed Monday
www.carlmarletti.com

Chez Bogato pages 36 and 119
• 7, rue Liancourt, 14ᵉ, 01 40 47 03 51,
closed Sunday and Monday
www.chezbogato.fr

**ChocoLatitudes
for Zotter and Bonnat pages 61 and 119**
• 57, rue Daguerre, 14ᵉ, 01 42 18 49 02,
closed Monday and Tuesday
www.chocolatitudes.com
Zotter : *www.zotter.at*

Bonnat : *www.bonnat-chocolatier.com*

Christophe Roussel page 70
• 10, rue du Champ-de-Mars, 7ᵉ,
01 40 62 67 00
• 5, rue Tardieu, 18ᵉ, 01 42 58 91 01
La Baule
• 6, allée des Camélias, 02 40 60 65 04
• 19, avenue Charles-de-Gaulle,
02 40 23 10 84
www.christophe-roussel.fr

Ciel page 106
• 3, rue Monge, 5ᵉ,
01 43 29 40 78, closed Monday
www.patisserie-ciel.com

Claudio Corallo page 61
• L'Arbre à Café, 10, rue du Nil, 2ᵉ,
closed Sunday and Monday
www.claudiocorallo.com
and www.larbreacafe.com

Colorova page 98
• 47, rue de l'Abbé-Grégoire, 6ᵉ,
01 45 44 67 56, closed Monday
'Colorova pâtisserie' on Facebook

Comme à Lisbonne page 24
• 37, rue du Roi-de-Sicile, 4ᵉ,
07 61 23 42 30, closed Monday
www.commealisbonne.com

Cuisine Attitude, Cyril Lignac page 119
• 10, cité Dupetit-Thouars, 03ᵉ,
01 49 96 00 50
www.cuisineattitude.com

D

Des Gâteaux & du Pain page 32
• 89, rue du Bac, 7ᵉ, closed Tuesday
• 63, boulevard Pasteur, 15ᵉ,
01 45 38 94 16, closed Tuesday
www.desgateauxetdupain.com

Didier Fourreau page 12
• 87, rue de Courcelles, 17ᵉ,
01 47 63 93 05, closed Sunday
www.didierfourreau.com

Dominique Saibron page 50
• 77, avenue du Général-Leclerc,
14ᵉ, 01 43 35 01 07, closed Monday
www.dominique-saibron.com

Du Pain and des Idées page 49
• 34, rue Yves-Toudic, 10ᵉ, 01 42 40 44 52,
closed Saturday and Sunday
www.dupainetdesidees.com

F

Fabrice Gillotte page 73
• Mococha, 89, rue Mouffetard, 5ᵉ,
01 47 07 13 66, closed Monday
www.chocolatsmococha.com
Dijon
• 21, rue du Bourg,
03 80 30 38 88, closed Sunday
www.fabrice-gillotte.fr

Franck Kestener page 59
• 7, rue Gay-Lussac, 5ᵉ, 01 43 26 40 91
Sarreguemines
• 6, rue Gutenberg,
03 87 28 14 62,
closed Sunday and Monday
www.franck-kestener.com

G

Gâteaux Thoumieux page 8
• 58, rue Saint-Dominique, 7ᵉ,
01 45 51 12 12, closed Tuesday
www.gateauxthoumieux.com

Gérard Mulot pages 11 and 42
• 6, rue du Pas-de-la-Mule, 3ᵉ,
01 42 78 52 17, closed Monday
• 76, rue de Seine and 2, rue Lobineau, 6ᵉ,
01 43 26 85 77, closed Wednesday
• 93, rue de la Glacière, 13ᵉ,
01 45 81 39 09, closed Monday
www.gerard-mulot.com

Gontran Cherrier page 42
• 8, rue Juliette-Lamber, 17ᵉ,
01 40 54 72 60, closed Wednesday
• 22, rue Caulaincourt, 18ᵉ,
01 46 06 82 66, closed Wednesday
• 1, rue de la Grande-Fontaine,
78100 Saint-Germain-en-Laye,
01 39 10 89 98, closed Thursday
www.gontrancherrierboulanger.com

Grom page 91
• 81, rue de Seine, 6ᵉ, 01 40 46 92 60
www.grom.it/fra

H

Helmut Newcake page 102
• 36, rue Bichat, 10ᵉ,
09 82 59 00 39, closed Monday and Tuesday
www.helmutnewcake.com

Henri Le Roux pages 70 and 84
• 1, rue de Bourbon-le-Château, 6ᵉ,
01 82 28 49 80
• 24, rue des Martyrs, 9ᵉ,
01 82 28 49 83, closed Monday
Quiberon
• 18, rue de Port-Maria, 02 97 50 06 83,
closed Sunday and Monday
www.chocolatleroux.com

Hugo & Victor pages 35 and 69
• 7, rue Gomboust, 1ᵉʳ, 01 42 96 10 20
• 40, boulevard Raspail, 7ᵉ, 01 44 39 97 73
• Printemps Haussmann,
64, boulevard Haussmann, 9ᵉ, 01 42 82 64 51,
closed Sunday
www.hugovictor.com

I

It Mylk page 88
• Galeries Lafayette, 48, bld Haussmann,
6th floor and terrace, 9ᵉ, closed Sunday
• 1, place Suzanne-Valadon, by the lower
funicular station, 18ᵉ, closed Monday
through Friday
• Aéroport de Roissy-Charles-de-Gaulle,
terminal 2E, Duty-Free Area, Gate L21-L23,
95700 Roissy-en-France
• Other points of sale (some temporary)
are listed on the website:
www.itmylk.fr

J

Jacques Genin pages 62, 83 and 98
• 133, rue de Turenne, 3ᵉ,
01 45 77 29 01, closed Monday
www.jacquesgenin.fr

Jean-Charles Rochoux page 56
• 16, rue d'Assas, 6ᵉ,
01 42 84 29 45, closed Sunday
www.jcrochoux.com

Jean-Paul Hévin pages 64 and 101
• 231, rue Saint-Honoré, 1ᵉʳ,
01 55 35 35 96, closed Sunday
• 3, rue Vavin, 6ᵉ,
01 43 54 09 85,
closed Sunday and Monday
• 23 bis, avenue de la Motte-Picquet, 7ᵉ,
01 45 51 77 48,
closed Sunday and Monday
• Lafayette Gourmet Haussmann,
48, boulevard Haussmann, 9ᵉ,
01 40 06 00 02,
closed Sunday
www.jeanpaulhevin.com

Jugetsudo page 106
• 95, rue de Seine, 6ᵉ,
01 46 33 94 90,
closed Sunday
www.jugetsudo.fr

K

Kaffeehaus page 109
• 11, rue Poncelet, 17ᵉ,
01 42 67 07 19,
closed Monday
www.kaffeehaus-paris.fr

L

Ladurée page 16
• 16-18, rue Royale, 8ᵉ,
01 42 60 21 79, open 7/7
• 75, avenue des Champs-Élysées, 8ᵉ,
01 40 75 08 75, open 7/7
• 21, rue Bonaparte, 6ᵉ,
01 44 07 64 87, open 7/7
• Printemps Haussmann, 1st Floor,
64, boulevard Haussmann, 9ᵉ,
01 42 82 40 10, closed Sunday
• Château de Versailles, 78000 Versailles,
01 30 83 04 02, closed Monday
• Paris Charles-de-Gaulle Airport,
Terminals AC, 2E, 2F, 95700
Roissy-en-France
• Paris Orly Airport, West Terminal, Hall 2,
91550 Orly, 01 74 22 07 77
www.laduree.com

La Fabrique à Gâteaux page 28
• 34, rue des Vinaigriers, 10ᵉ,
09 83 26 68 02, closed Monday and Tuesday
'La Fabrique à Gâteaux' on Facebook

La Gambette à Pain page 49
• 86, avenue Gambetta, 20ᵉ, 01 43 64 52 34,
closed Saturday and Sunday
'La Gambette À Pain Marque déposée'
on Facebook

La Gazelle d'Or page 19
44, rue Olivier de Serres, 15ᵉ,
01 40 45 02 07, closed Saturday
www.lagazelle-dor.com

La Maison du Chocolat pages 36 and 74
• Carrousel du Louvre,
99, rue de Rivoli, 1ᵉʳ, 01 42 97 13 50
• 19, rue de Sèvres, 6ᵉ, 01 45 44 20 40
• 225, rue du Faubourg-Saint-Honoré, 8ᵉ,
01 42 27 39 44
• 52, rue François-Iᵉʳ, 8ᵉ,
01 47 23 38 25, closed Sunday
• 8, boulevard de la Madeleine,
9ᵉ, 01 47 42 86 52
• Printemps Haussmann,
64, boulevard Haussmann, 9ᵉ,
01 42 82 61 77, closed Sunday
• 120, avenue Victor-Hugo, 16ᵉ,
01 40 67 77 83
• La Vallée Village, 3, cours de la Garonne,
77700 Serris
• Parly-2, Level 1, porte Opéra,
2, avenue Charles-de-Gaulle,
78150 Le Chesnay, closed Sunday
• Orly Airport, Terminal Ouest, Hall 2, porte
A, 91550 Orly, 01 49 75 11 10
• Charles-de-Gaulle Airport,
Terminals 2A-2C, 2E, 2F,
95700 Roissy-en-France
www.lamaisonduchocolat.fr

La Maison du Chou page 101
• 7, rue de Furstenberg, 6ᵉ,
09 54 75 06 05, closed Monday
'La Maison du Chou' on Facebook

La Manufacture de Chocolat
d'Alain Ducasse pages 55 and 62
• 26, rue Saint-Benoît, 6ᵉ,
01 45 48 87 89, closed Monday
• Galeries Lafayette Maison,
35, boulevard Haussmann, 9ᵉ,
01 42 65 48 26, closed Sunday
• 40, rue de la Roquette, 11ᵉ, 01 48 05 82 86,
closed Sunday and Monday
www.lechocolat-alainducasse.com

La Pâtisserie by Cyril Lignac pages 12 and 46
• 24, rue Paul-Bert, 11ᵉ, 01 43 72 74 88
• 2, rue de Chaillot, 16ᵉ, 01 47 20 64 51
www.lapatisseriebycyrillignac.com

La Pâtisserie de l'Église page 16
10, rue du Jourdain, 20ᵉ,
01 46 36 66 08, open 7/7
www.demoncyvergne.com

La Pâtisserie des Rêves pages 31 and 102
• 93, rue du Bac, 7ᵉ,
01 42 84 00 82, closed Monday
• Centre commercial Beaugrenelle,
12, rue Linois, 15ᵉ,
01 45 77 27 49 ou 01 45 77 28 32
• 111, rue de Longchamp, 16ᵉ,
01 47 04 00 24, closed Monday
• 19, rue Poncelet, 17ᵉ,
01 42 67 71 79, closed Monday
• Parly-2, 78158 Le Chesnay,
01 39 02 08 63, closed Sunday
www.lapatisseriedesreves.com

La Petite Rose page 11
• 11, boulevard de Courcelles, 8ᵉ,
01 45 22 07 27, closed Monday

L'Atelier des Chefs page 116
• 8, rue Pernelle, 4ᵉ, 01 44 54 39 10
• 10, rue de Penthièvre, 8ᵉ, 01 53 30 05 82
• Galeries Lafayette Maison,
35, boulevard Haussmann, 9ᵉ, 01 49 70 97 50
• 20, rue Saint-Lazare, 9ᵉ, 01 49 70 97 50
• 162, avenue de France, 13ᵉ, 01 44 97 01 86
• 27, rue Péclet, 15ᵉ, 01 56 08 33 50
• Printemps Nation, 21, cours de Vincennes,
20ᵉ, 01 49 70 97 50
www.atelierdeschefs.fr

L'Atelier des Sens page 119
- 10, rue du Bourg-l'Abbé, 3ᵉ, 01 40 21 08 50
- 32, rue Vignon, 9ᵉ, 01 40 21 08 50
- 40, rue Sedaine, 11ᵉ, 01 40 21 08 50
www.atelier-des-sens.com

La Tropicale page 95
- 180, boulevard Vincent-Auriol, 13ᵉ,
01 42 16 87 27, closed Sunday
www.latropicaleglacier.com

L'Autre Boulange page 50
- 43, rue de Montreuil, 11ᵉ,
01 43 72 86 04, closed Sunday and Monday
- 12, place de la Nation, 12ᵉ,
01 43 43 41 30, closed Sunday and Monday

Le Bac à Glaces page 91
- 109, rue du Bac, 7ᵉ,
01 45 48 87 65, closed Sunday
www.bacaglaces.com

Le Cacaotier page 65
- 44, rue de Verneuil, 7ᵉ, 01 49 27 92 43,
closed Sunday and Monday
- 14, rue de Mora, 95880 Enghien-les-Bains,
01 39 89 29 31, closed Sunday and Monday
www.lecacaotier.com

L'Éclair de Génie page 12
- 14, rue Pavée, 4ᵉ,
01 42 77 85 11, closed Monday
- Passy Plaza, 53, rue de Passy, 16ᵉ,
09 72 30 59 72, closed Monday
www.leclairdegenie.com

L'École de Cuisine Alain Ducasse page 116
- 64, rue du Ranelagh, 16ᵉ, 01 44 90 91 00
www.ecolecuisine-alainducasse.com

Le Comptoir Baulois page 23
- 34, rue Godot-de-Mauroy, 9ᵉ,
01 40 06 04 18, closed Sunday
La Baule
- 131, avenue du Général-de-Gaulle,
02 40 23 16 05, closed Monday
www.lefondantbaulois.com

Le Royal Monceau page 113
- 37, avenue Hoche, 8ᵉ, 01 42 99 88 00
www.leroyalmonceau.com

Liberté, Boulangerie-Pâtisserie by Benoît Castel page 11
- 39, rue des Vinaigriers, 10ᵉ,
01 42 05 51 76, closed Sunday
"Liberté by Benoît Castel" on Facebook

Librairie Gourmande page 116
- 92-96, rue Montmartre, 2ᵉ, 01 43 54 37 27,
closed Sunday
www.librairiegourmande.fr

M

Maison Landemaine page 45
- 56, rue de Clichy, 9ᵉ,
01 48 74 37 64, closed Monday
- 26, rue des Martyrs, 9ᵉ,
01 40 16 03 42, closed Monday
- 121, rue de Charonne, 11ᵉ,
01 43 71 33 06, closed Wednesday
- 130, rue de la Roquette, 11ᵉ,
01 43 79 98 03, closed Monday
- 136, rue de la Roquette, 11ᵉ,
01 43 79 65 98, closed Monday
- 2, rue Crozatier, 12ᵉ,
01 43 43 80 50, closed Monday
- 4, rue du Poteau, 18ᵉ,
01 42 64 87 78, closed Sunday
www.maisonlandemaine.com

Maison Pralus pages 46 and 56
- 35, rue Rambuteau, 4ᵉ, 01 57 40 84 55
- 44, rue Cler, 7ᵉ, 01 45 56 13 75
Roanne
- Les Halles Diderot, 04 77 67 69 02,
closed Monday
- 8, rue Charles-de-Gaulle, 04 77 71 24 10,
closed Sunday and Monday
www.chocolats-pralus.com

Martine Lambert page 95
• 39, rue Cler, 7ᵉ,
01 40 62 97 18, closed Monday and Tuesday
Deauville
• 76 bis, rue Eugène-Colas, 02 31 88 94 04
www.martine-lambert.com

Meert page 20
• 16, rue Elzévir, 3ᵉ,
01 49 96 56 90, closed Monday
• 3, rue Jacques-Callot, 6ᵉ,
01 56 81 67 15, closed Monday
Lille
• 27, rue Esquermoise,
03 20 57 07 44, closed Monday
www.meert.fr

Michalak Master Class page 116
• 60, rue du Faubourg-Poissonnière, 10ᵉ,
01 42 46 10 45, closed Sunday and Monday
www.christophemichalak.com

Mister Ice page 92
• 6, rue Descombes, 17ᵉ, 01 42 67 76 24,
closed Sunday and Monday
www.glacier-foenix.com

Mori Yoshida pages 15 and 50
• 65, avenue de Breteuil, 7ᵉ,
01 47 34 29 74, closed Monday
www.moriyoshida.fr

P

Pain de Sucre pages 35 and 80
• 14, rue Rambuteau, 3ᵉ, 01 45 74 68 92,
closed Tuesday and Wednesday
www.patisseriepaindesucre.com

Pariès pages 23 and 83
• 9 bis, rue Saint-Placide, 06ᵉ, 01 45 44 64 64
Saint-Jean-de-Luz
• 9, rue Gambetta, 05 59 26 01 46
www.paries.fr

Pastelaria Belem page 109
• 47, rue Boursault, 17ᵉ,
01 45 22 38 95, closed Monday

Pâtisserie des Martyrs pages 8, 46 and 80
• 22, rue des Martyrs, 9ᵉ,
01 71 18 24 70, closed Monday
www.sebastiengaudard.com

Patrick Roger pages 55 and 74
• 108, boulevard Saint-Germain, 6ᵉ,
09 63 64 50 21
• 91, rue de Rennes, 6ᵉ,
01 45 44 66 13, closed Sunday
• 3, place de la Madeleine, 8ᵉ, 01 42 65 24 47
• 199, rue du Faubourg-Saint-Honoré, 8ᵉ,
01 45 61 11 46, closed Sunday
• 45, avenue Victor-Hugo, 16ᵉ,
01 45 01 66 71, closed Sunday
• 2, rue de Paris, 78100 Saint-Germain-en-
Laye, 01 34 51 72 85, closed Monday
• 47, rue Houdan, 92330 Sceaux,
01 47 02 30 17, closed Monday
Brussels
• Place du Grand-Sablon, 43,
(0032) 2 514 70 46
www.patrickroger.com

Pierre Hermé pages 28 and 65
• 4, rue Cambon, 1ᵉʳ, 01 43 54 47 77
• 39, avenue de l'Opéra, 2ᵉ, 01 43 54 47 77
• 18, rue Sainte-Croix-de-la-Bretonnerie,
04ᵉ, 01 43 54 47 77
• 72, rue Bonaparte, 6ᵉ, 01 43 54 47 77
• 89, boulevard Malesherbes, 8ᵉ,
01 43 54 47 77
• Publicis Drugstore, 133, avenue des
Champs-Élysées, 8ᵉ, 01 43 54 47 77
• Galeries Lafayette,
40, boulevard Haussmann, 9ᵉ,
01 43 54 47 77, closed Sunday
• 185, rue de Vaugirard, 15ᵉ, 01 47 83 89 97
• 58, avenue Paul-Doumer, 16ᵉ,
01 43 54 47 77
• Parly-2, avenue Charles-de-Gaulle,
78150 Le Chesnay, 01 43 54 47 77,
closed Sunday
www.pierreherme.com

Pierre Marcolini page 59
• 89, rue de Seine, 6e,
01 44 07 39 07, closed Sunday
• 78, rue du Bac, 7e,
01 45 44 34 02, closed Sunday
• 3, rue Scribe, 9e,
01 44 71 03 74, closed Sunday
Brussels
• Avenue de Hinnisdael, 14,
(0032) 2 771 27 20, closed Sunday
• Boulevard de la Woluwe, 28,
(0032) 2 771 20 60
• Chaussée de Waterloo, 1302,
(0032) 2 372 15 11, closed Sunday
• Cour Wiltcher's, avenue Louise, 75 M,
(0032) 2 538 42 24, closed Sunday
• Gare Eurostar, rue de France, 2,
(0032) 2 523 58 97
• Galerie de la Reine, 21,
(0032) 2 502 35 67
• Place du Grand-Sablon, 39,
(0032) 2 513 17 83, closed Monday
• Rue des Minimes 1, place du Grand-Sablon,
(0032) 2 514 12 06
www.marcolini.com

Plaza Athénée page 110
• 25, avenue Montaigne, 8e,
01 53 67 66 00
www.plaza-athenee-paris.fr

Popelini page 15
• 29, rue Debelleyme, 3e,
01 44 61 31 44, closed Monday
• 44, rue des Martyrs, 9e,
01 42 81 35 79, closed Monday
www.popelini.com

Pozzetto page 88
• 16, rue Vieille-du-Temple, 3e,
01 42 77 08 64
• 39, rue du Roi-de-Sicile, 4e, 01 42 77 08 64
www.pozzetto.biz

Prince de Galles page 113
• 33, avenue George-V, 8e,
01 53 23 78 52
www.bar-les-heures.fr

R

Rachel's Cakes page 24
• 25, rue du Pont-aux-Choux, 3e,
01 41 63 28 80 (number for the lab in
Montreuil), closed Monday
www.rachelscakes.fr

Raimo page 95
• 17, rue des Archives, 4e, 01 48 87 24 61,
closed Monday
• 65, boulevard Saint-Germain, 5e,
01 46 34 36 59, closed Sunday and Monday
• 63, boulevard de Reuilly, 12e,
01 43 43 70 17, closed Monday
www.raimo.fr

Régis page 76
• 89, rue de Passy, 16e,
01 45 27 70 00, closed Sunday afternoon and
Monday morning

S

Sadaharu Aoki pages 36 and 73
• 56, boulevard de Port-Royal, 5e,
01 45 35 36 80, closed Monday
• 35, rue de Vaugirard, 6e,
01 45 44 48 90, closed Monday
• Lafayette Gourmet,
40, boulevard Haussmann, 9e,
01 40 23 52 67, closed Sunday
• 25, rue Pérignon, 15e,
01 43 06 02 71, closed Sunday
www.sadaharuaoki.com

Salon du chocolat page 73
• Viparis, porte de Versailles, 15e
www.salonduchocolat.fr

Scoop Me a Cookie page 19
• 5-7, rue Crespin du Gast, 11e,
01 73 74 28 90, closed Monday
www.scoopmeacookie.com

Sébastien Dégardin,
la Pâtisserie du Panthéon page 32
• 200, rue Saint-Jacques, 5ᵉ, 01 43 07 77 59,
closed Monday and Tuesday
www.sebastien-degardin.com

Shangri-La page 110
• 10, avenue d'Iéna, 16ᵉ, 01 53 67 19 98
www.shangri-la.com

She's Cake page 106
• 20, avenue Ledru-Rollin, 12ᵉ,
01 53 46 93 16, closed Monday
www.shescake.fr

Stéphane Vandermeersch page 45
• 278, avenue Daumesnil, 12ᵉ,
01 43 47 21 66,
closed Monday and Tuesday
www.boulangerie-patisserie-vandermeersch.com

Sugarplum Cake Shop page 106
• 68, rue du Cardinal-Lemoine, 5ᵉ,
01 46 34 07 43,
closed Monday
www.sugarplumcakeshop.com

T
Toraya page 105
• 10, rue Saint-Florentin, 1ᵉʳ,
01 42 60 13 00,
closed Sunday
www.toraya-group.co.jp/paris

W
Walaku page 105
• 33, rue Rousselet, 7ᵉ,
01 56 24 11 02,
closed Monday and Tuesday
www.walaku-paris.com

1 T. Rue Scribe page 102
• 1, rue Scribe, 9ᵉ,
01 44 71 24 03
www.hotel-scribe.com

Addresses
By Arrondissement and By City

1st arrondissement
Aki Boulangerie page 45
16, rue Sainte-Anne,
01 40 15 63 38, closed Sunday

Hugo & Victor pages 35 and 69
7, rue Gomboust, 01 42 96 10 20
www.hugovictor.com

Jean-Paul Hévin pages 66 and 101
231, rue Saint-Honoré,
01 55 35 35 96, closed Sunday
www.jeanpaulhevin.com

La Maison du Chocolat pages 36 and 74
Carrousel du Louvre,
99, rue de Rivoli, 01 42 97 13 50
www.lamaisonduchocolat.fr

Pierre Hermé pages 28 and 65
4, rue Cambon, 01 43 54 47 77
www.pierreherme.com

Toraya page 105
10, rue Saint-Florentin,
01 42 60 13 00, closed Sunday
www.toraya-group.co.jp/paris

2nd arrondissement
À la Mère de Famille pages 69 and 92
82, rue Montorgueil, 01 53 40 82 78
www.lameredefamille.com

Claudio Corallo page 61
L'Arbre à Café, 10, rue du Nil,
closed Sunday and Monday
www.claudiocorallo.com
and www.larbreacafe.com

Librairie Gourmande page 116
92-96, rue Montmartre,
01 43 54 37 27, closed Sunday
www.librairiegourmande.fr

Pierre Hermé pages 28 and 65
39, avenue de l'Opéra,
01 43 54 47 77
www.pierreherme.com

3rd arrondissement
Café Pouchkine page 31
2, rue des Francs-Bourgeois,
01 42 72 97 05, open 7/7
www.cafe-pouchkine.fr

Carette page 101
25, place des Vosges,
01 48 87 94 07
www.carette-paris.com

Gérard Mulot pages 11 and 42
6, rue du Pas-de-la-Mule,
01 42 78 52 17, closed Monday
www.gerard-mulot.com

Jacques Genin pages 62, 83 and 98
133, rue de Turenne,
01 45 77 29 01, closed Monday
www.jacquesgenin.fr

L'Atelier des Sens page 119
10, rue du Bourg-l'Abbé,
01 40 21 08 50
www.atelier-des-sens.com

Cuisine Attitude, Cyril Lignac page 119
10, cité Dupetit-Thouars,
01 49 96 00 50
www.cuisineattitude.com

Meert page 16
16, rue Elzévir,
01 49 96 56 90, closed Monday
www.meert.fr

Pain de Sucre pages 39 and 80
14, rue Rambuteau, 01 45 74 68 92,
closed Tuesday and Wednesday
www.patisseriepaindesucre.com

Popelini page 15
29, rue Debelleyme,
01 44 61 31 44, closed Monday
www.popelini.com

Pozzetto page 88
16, rue Vieille-du-Temple,
01 42 77 08 64
www.pozzetto.biz

Rachel's Cakes page 24
25, rue du Pont-aux-Choux,
01 41 63 28 80 (number for the lab in
Montreuil), closed Monday
www.rachelscakes.fr

4th arrondissement
Benoît Chocolats page 76
75, rue Saint-Antoine,
01 49 96 52 02, closed Sunday
www.chocolats-benoit.com

Berthillon page 91
31, rue Saint-Louis-en-l'Île,
01 43 54 31 61, closed Monday and Tuesday
www.berthillon.fr

Comme à Lisbonne page 24
37, rue du Roi-de-Sicile,
07 61 23 42 30, closed Monday
www.commealisbonne.com

L'Atelier des Chefs page 116
8, rue Pernelle, 01 44 54 39 10
www.atelierdeschefs.fr

L'Éclair de Génie page 12
14, rue Pavée,
01 42 77 85 11, closed Monday
www.leclairdegenie.com

Maison Pralus pages 46 and 56
35, rue Rambuteau, 01 57 40 84 55
www.chocolats-pralus.com

Pierre Hermé pages 28 and 65
18, rue Sainte-Croix-de-la-Bretonnerie,
01 43 54 47 77
www.pierreherme.com

Pozzetto page 88
39, rue du Roi-de-Sicile, 01 42 77 08 64
www.pozzetto.biz

Raimo page 95
17, rue des Archives, 01 48 87 24 61
closed Monday
www.raimo.fr

5th arrondissement
Aux Merveilleux de Fred page 20
2, rue Monge, 01 43 54 63 72, closed Monday
www.auxmerveilleux.com

Carl Marletti page 8
51, rue Censier, 01 43 31 68 12, closed Monday
www.carlmarletti.com

Ciel page 106
3, rue Monge, 01 43 29 40 78, closed Monday
www.patisserie-ciel.com

Fabrice Gillotte page 73
Mococha, 89, rue Mouffetard,
01 47 07 13 66, closed Monday
www.chocolatsmococha.com

Franck Kestener page 59
7, rue Gay-Lussac, 01 43 26 40 91
www.franck-kestener.com

Raimo page 95
65, boulevard Saint-Germain,
01 46 34 36 59, closed Sunday
and Monday
www.raimo.fr

Sadaharu Aoki pages 39 and 73
56, boulevard de Port-Royal,
01 45 35 36 80, closed Monday
www.sadaharuaoki.com

**Sébastien Dégardin,
la Pâtisserie du Panthéon page 32**
200, rue Saint-Jacques, 01 43 07 77 59,
closed Monday and Tuesday
www.sebastien-degardin.com

Sugarplum Cake Shop page 106
68, rue du Cardinal-Lemoine,
01 46 34 07 43, closed Monday
www.sugarplumcakeshop.com

6th arrondissement
À la Mère de Famille pages 69 and 92
• 70, rue Bonaparte, (not yet open at the
time of printing)
• 39, rue du Cherche-Midi,
01 42 22 49 99, closed Sunday
www.lameredefamille.com

Arnaud Larher pages 36 and 66
93, rue de Seine,
01 43 29 38 15, closed Monday
www.arnaud-larher.com

Bread & Roses page 24
62, rue Madame,
01 42 22 06 06, closed Sunday
www.breadandroses.fr

Colorova page 98
47, rue de l'Abbé-Grégoire,
01 45 44 67 56, closed Monday
'Colorova pâtisserie' on Facebook

Gérard Mulot pages 11 and 42
76, rue de Seine and 2, rue Lobineau,
01 43 26 85 77, closed Wednesday
www.gerard-mulot.com

Grom page 91
81, rue de Seine, 01 40 46 92 60
www.grom.it/fra

Henri Le Roux pages 70 and 84
1, rue de Bourbon-le-Château, 01 82 28 49 80
www.chocolatleroux.com

Jean-Charles Rochoux page 56
16, rue d'Assas,
01 42 84 29 45, closed Sunday
www.jcrochoux.com

Jean-Paul Hévin pages 66 and 101
3, rue Vavin, 01 43 54 09 85,
closed Sunday and Monday
www.jeanpaulhevin.com

Joséphine Bakery page 8
42, rue Jacob, 01 42 60 20 39,
closed Sunday
'Joséphine Bakery' on Facebook

Jugetsudo page 106
95, rue de Seine, 01 46 33 94 90,
closed Sunday
www.jugetsudo.fr

La Maison du Chocolat pages 36 and 74
19, rue de Sèvres, 01 45 44 20 40
www.lamaisonduchocolat.fr

La Maison du Chou page 101
7, rue de Furstenberg,
09 54 75 06 05, closed Monday
'La Maison du Chou' on Facebook

La Manufacture de Chocolat d'Alain Ducasse pages 55 et 62
26, rue Saint-Benoît, 01 45 48 87 89,
closed Monday
www.lechocolat-alainducasse.com

Meert page 20
3, rue Jacques-Callot,
01 56 81 67 15, closed Monday
www.meert.fr

Pariès pages 23 and 83
9 bis, rue Saint-Placide, 01 45 44 64 64
www.paries.fr

Patrick Roger pages 55 and 74
• 108, bld Saint-Germain, 09 63 64 50 21
• 91, rue de Rennes, 01 45 44 66 13,
closed Sunday
www.patrickroger.com

Pierre Hermé pages 28 and 65
72, rue Bonaparte, 01 43 54 47 77
www.pierreherme.com

Pierre Marcolini page 59
89, rue de Seine, 01 44 07 39 07,
closed Sunday
www.marcolini.com

Sadaharu Aoki pages 39 and 73
35, rue de Vaugirard,
01 45 44 48 90, closed Monday
www.sadaharuaoki.com

7ᵗʰ arrondissement

À la Mère de Famille pages 69 and 92
47, rue Cler, 01 45 55 29 74, closed Monday
www.lameredefamille.com

Aux Merveilleux de Fred page 20
94, rue Saint-Dominique,
01 47 53 91 34, closed Monday
www.auxmerveilleux.com

Christophe Roussel page 70
10, rue du Champ-de-Mars, 01 40 62 67 00
www.christophe-roussel.fr

Des Gâteaux & du Pain page 32
89, rue du Bac, closed Tuesday
www.desgateauxetdupain.com

Gâteaux Thoumieux page 8
58, rue Saint-Dominique,
01 45 51 12 12, closed Tuesday
www.gateauxthoumieux.com

Hugo & Victor pages 35 and 69
40, boulevard Raspail, 01 44 39 97 73
www.hugovictor.com

Jean-Paul Hévin pages 66 and 101
23 bis, avenue de la Motte-Picquet,
01 45 51 77 48,
closed Sunday and Monday
www.jeanpaulhevin.com

La Pâtisserie des Rêves pages 31 and 102
93, rue du Bac, 01 42 84 00 82,
closed Monday
www.lapatisseriedesreves.com

Le Bac à Glaces page 91
109, rue du Bac, 01 45 48 87 65,
closed Sunday
www.bacaglaces.com

Le Cacaotier page 65
44, rue de Verneuil, 01 49 27 92 43,
closed Sunday and Monday
www.lecacaotier.com

Maison Pralus pages 46 and 56
44, rue Cler, 01 45 56 13 75
www.chocolats-pralus.com

Martine Lambert page 95
39, rue Cler, 01 40 62 97 18,
closed Monday and Tuesday
www.martine-lambert.com

Mori Yoshida pages 15 and 50
65, avenue de Breteuil,
01 47 34 29 74, closed Monday
www.moriyoshida.fr

Pierre Marcolini page 59
78, rue du Bac, 01 45 44 34 02,
closed Sunday
www.marcolini.com

Walaku page 105
33, rue Rousselet, 01 56 24 11 02,
closed Monday and Tuesday
www.walaku-paris.com

8th arrondissement
Bread & Roses page 24
25, rue Boissy-d'Anglas,
01 47 42 40 00, closed Sunday
www.breadandroses.fr

Ladurée page 16
• 16-18, rue Royale, 01 42 60 21 79
• 75, avenue des Champs-Élysées,
01 40 75 08 75
www.laduree.com

La Maison du Chocolat pages 36 and 74
• 225, rue du Faubourg-Saint-Honoré,
01 42 27 39 44
• 52, rue François-Ier, 01 47 23 38 25,
closed Sunday
www.lamaisonduchocolat.fr

La Petite Rose page 11
11, boulevard de Courcelles,
01 45 22 07 27, closed Monday

L'Atelier des Chefs page 116
10, rue de Penthièvre, 01 53 30 05 82
www.atelierdeschefs.fr

Le Royal Monceau page 113
37, avenue Hoche, 01 42 99 88 00
www.leroyalmonceau.com

Patrick Roger pages 55 and 74
• 3, place de la Madeleine, 01 42 65 24 47
• 199, rue du Faubourg-Saint-Honoré,
01 45 61 11 46, closed Sunday
www.patrickroger.com

Pierre Hermé pages 28 and 65
• 89, boulevard Malesherbes, 01 43 54 47 77
• Publicis Drugstore,
133, avenue des Champs-Élysées,
01 43 54 47 77
www.pierreherme.com

Plaza Athénée page 110
25, avenue Montaigne, 01 53 67 66 00
www.plaza-athenee-paris.fr

Prince de Galles page 113
33, avenue George-V, 01 53 23 78 52
www.bar-les-heures.fr

9th arrondissement
À la Mère de Famille pages 69 and 92
• 33 and 35, rue du Faubourg-Montmartre,
01 47 70 83 69
• Printemps Haussmann,
64, boulevard Haussmann,
01 42 82 49 56, closed Sunday
www.lameredefamille.com

Baillardran page 23
12, boulevard des Capucines,
01 47 42 39 88, closed Sunday
www.baillardran.com

Café Pouchkine page 31
Printemps de la mode,
64, boulevard Haussmann,
01 42 82 43 31, closed Sunday
www.cafe-pouchkine.fr

Henri Le Roux pages 70 and 84
24, rue des Martyrs, 01 82 28 49 83,
closed Monday
www.chocolatleroux.com

Hugo & Victor pages 35 and 69
Printemps Haussmann,
64, boulevard Haussmann,
01 42 82 64 51, closed Sunday
www.hugovictor.com

It Mylk page 88
Galeries Lafayette, 48, bld Haussmann,
6th floor, closed Sunday
www.itmylk.fr

Jean-Paul Hévin pages 66 and 101
Lafayette Gourmet Haussmann,
48, bld Haussmann, 01 40 06 00 02,
closed Sunday
www.jeanpaulhevin.com

Ladurée page 16
• Printemps Haussmann, 1st Floor,
64, boulevard Haussmann,
01 42 82 40 10, closed Sunday
www.laduree.com

La Maison du Chocolat pages 36 and 74
• 8, boulevard de la Madeleine, 01 47 42 86 52
• Printemps Haussmann,
64, boulevard Haussmann,
01 42 82 61 77, closed Sunday
www.lamaisonduchocolat.fr

**La Manufacture de Chocolat
d'Alain Ducasse pages 55 and 62**
Galeries Lafayette Maison,
35, boulevard Haussmann,
01 42 65 48 26, closed Sunday
www.lechocolat-alainducasse.com

L'Atelier des Chefs page 116
Galeries Lafayette Maison,
• 35, boulevard Haussmann, 01 49 70 97 50
• 20, rue Saint-Lazare, 01 49 70 97 50
www.atelierdeschefs.fr

L'Atelier des Sens page 119
32, rue Vignon, 01 40 21 08 50
www.atelier-des-sens.com

Le Comptoir Baulois page 23
34, rue Godot-de-Mauroy,
01 40 06 04 18, closed Sunday
www.lefondantbaulois.com

Maison Landemaine page 49
• 56, rue de Clichy,
01 48 74 37 64, closed Monday
• 26, rue des Martyrs,
01 40 16 03 42, closed Monday
www.maisonlandemaine.com

Pâtisserie des Martyrs pages 8, 46 and 80
22, rue des Martyrs,
01 71 18 24 70, closed Monday
www.sebastiengaudard.com

Pierre Hermé pages 28 and 65
Galeries Lafayette, 40, bld Haussmann,
01 43 54 47 77, closed Sunday
www.pierreherme.com

Pierre Marcolini page 59
3, rue Scribe,
01 44 71 03 74, closed Sunday
www.marcolini.com

Popelini page 15
44, rue des Martyrs,
01 42 81 35 79, closed Monday
www.popelini.com

Sadaharu Aoki pages 39 and 73
Lafayette Gourmet, 40, bld Haussmann,
01 40 23 52 67, closed Sunday
www.sadaharuaoki.com

1 T. Rue Scribe page 102
1, rue Scribe, 01 44 71 24 03
www.hotel-scribe.com

10ᵗʰ arrondissement

Du Pain and des Idées page 49
34, rue Yves-Toudic, 01 42 40 44 52,
closed Saturday and Sunday
www.dupainetdesidees.com

Helmut Newcake page 102
36, rue Bichat, 09 82 59 00 39,
closed Monday and Tuesday
www.helmutnewcake.com

La Fabrique à Gâteaux page 28
34, rue des Vinaigriers, 09 83 26 68 02,
closed Monday and Tuesday
'La Fabrique à Gâteaux' on Facebook

Liberté, Boulangerie-Pâtisserie by Benoît Castel page 11
39, rue des Vinaigriers,
01 42 05 51 76, closed Sunday
« Liberté par Benoît Castel » sur Facebook

Michalak Master Class page 116
60, rue du Faubourg-Poissonnière,
01 42 46 10 45,
closed Sunday and Monday
www.christophemichalak.com

11ᵗʰ arrondissement

La Manufacture de Chocolat d'Alain Ducasse pages 55 and 62
40, rue de la Roquette, 01 48 05 82 86,
closed Sunday and Monday
www.lechocolat-alainducasse.com

La Pâtisserie by Cyril Lignac pages 12 and 46
24, rue Paul-Bert, 01 43 72 74 88
www.lapatisseriebycyrillignac.com

L'Atelier des Sens page 119
40, rue Sedaine, 01 40 21 08 50
www.atelier-des-sens.com

L'Autre Boulange page 50
43, rue de Montreuil, 01 43 72 86 04,
closed Sunday and Monday

Maison Landemaine page 49
• 121, rue de Charonne,
01 43 71 33 06, closed Wednesday
• 130, rue de la Roquette,
01 43 79 98 03, closed Monday
• 136, rue de la Roquette,
01 43 79 65 98, closed Monday
www.maisonlandemaine.com

Scoop Me a Cookie page 19
5-7, rue Crespin du Gast,
01 73 74 28 90, closed Monday
www.scoopmeacookie.com

12ᵗʰ arrondissement

Blé Sucré page 35
7, rue Antoine-Vollon,
01 43 40 77 73, closed Monday
www.blesucre.fr

L'Autre Boulange page 50
12, place de la Nation,
01 43 43 41 30, closed Sunday and Monday

Maison Landemaine page 49
2, rue Crozatier,
01 43 43 80 50, closed Monday
www.maisonlandemaine.com

Raimo page 95
63, boulevard de Reuilly,
01 43 43 70 17, closed Monday
www.raimo.fr

She's Cake page 106
20, avenue Ledru-Rollin,
01 53 46 93 16, closed Monday
www.shescake.fr

Stéphane Vandermeersch page 45
278, avenue Daumesnil,
01 43 47 21 66, closed Monday and Tuesday
www.boulangerie-patisserie-vandermeersch.com

13th arrondissement

Gérard Mulot pages 11 and 42
93, rue de la Glacière,
01 45 81 39 09, closed Monday
www.gerard-mulot.com

L'Atelier des Chefs page 116
162, avenue de France, 01 44 97 01 86
www.atelierdeschefs.fr

La Tropicale page 95
180, boulevard Vincent-Auriol,
01 42 16 87 27, closed Sunday
www.latropicaleglacier.com

14th arrondissement

Baillardran page 23
Gare Montparnasse, Bâtiment Voyageur,
level C, in front of Track 13, 01 40 47 99 24
www.baillardran.com

Chez Bogato pages 36 and 119
7, rue Liancourt, 01 40 47 03 51,
closed Sunday and Monday
www.chezbogato.fr

**ChocoLatitudes
pour Zotter et Bonnat pages 61 and 119**
57, rue Daguerre, 01 42 18 49 02,
closed Monday and Tuesday
www.chocolatitudes.com
Zotter : *www.zotter.at*
Bonnat : *www.bonnat-chocolatier.com*

Dominique Saibron page 50
77, avenue du Général-Leclerc,
01 43 35 01 07, closed Monday
www.dominique-saibron.com

15th arrondissement

Aux Merveilleux de Fred page 20
129 bis, rue Saint-Charles,
01 45 79 72 47, closed Monday
www.auxmerveilleux.com

Des Gâteaux & du Pain page 32
63, boulevard Pasteur,
01 45 38 94 16, closed Tuesday
www.desgateauxetdupain.com

La Gazelle d'Or page 19
44, rue Olivier de Serres,
01 40 45 02 07, closed Saturday
www.lagazelle-dor.com

La Pâtisserie des Rêves pages 31 and 102
Centre commercial Beaugrenelle,
12, rue Linois,
01 45 77 27 49 ou 01 45 77 28 32
www.lapatisseriedesreves.com

L'Atelier des Chefs page 116
27, rue Péclet, 01 56 08 33 50
www.atelierdeschefs.fr

Pierre Hermé pages 28 and 65
185, rue de Vaugirard, 01 47 83 89 97
www.pierreherme.com

Sadaharu Aoki pages 39 and 73
25, rue Pérignon,
01 43 06 02 71, closed Sunday
www.sadaharuaoki.com

Salon du chocolat page 73
Viparis, porte de Versailles
www.salonduchocolat.fr

16th arrondissement

À la Mère de Famille pages 69 and 92
59, rue de la Pompe, 01 45 04 73 19
www.lameredefamille.com

Aux Merveilleux de Fred page 20
29, rue de l'Annonciation,
01 45 20 13 82, closed Monday
www.auxmerveilleux.com

Carette page 101
4, place du Trocadéro, 01 47 27 98 85
www.carette-paris.com

La Maison du Chocolat pages 36 and 74
120, avenue Victor-Hugo, 01 40 67 77 83
www.lamaisonduchocolat.fr

La Pâtisserie by Cyril Lignac pages 12 and 46
2, rue de Chaillot, 01 47 20 64 51
www.lapatisseriebycyrillignac.com

La Pâtisserie des Rêves pages 31 and 102
111, rue de Longchamp,
01 47 04 00 24, closed Monday
www.lapatisseriedesreves.com

L'Éclair de Génie page 12
Passy Plaza, 53, rue de Passy,
09 72 30 59 72, closed Monday
www.leclairdegenie.com

L'École de Cuisine Alain Ducasse page 116
64, rue du Ranelagh, 01 44 90 91 00
www.ecolecuisine-alainducasse.com

Patrick Roger pages 55 and 74
45, avenue Victor-Hugo,
01 45 01 66 71, closed Sunday
www.patrickroger.com

Pierre Hermé pages 28 and 65
58, avenue Paul-Doumer, 01 43 54 47 77
www.pierreherme.com

Régis page 76
89, rue de Passy,
01 45 27 70 00, closed Sunday afternoon and
Monday morning

Shangri-La page 110
10, avenue d'Iéna, 01 53 67 19 98
www.shangri-la.com

17th arrondissement
Acide Salon de thé page 98
24, rue des Moines,
09 83 87 05 09, closed Monday
www.acidemacaron.com

À la Mère de Famille pages 69 and 92
• 107, rue Jouffroy-d'Abbans,
01 47 63 15 15, closed Sunday
• 30, rue Legendre, 01 47 63 52 94
www.lameredefamille.com

Aux Merveilleux de Fred page 20
7, rue de Tocqueville,
01 42 27 86 63, closed Monday
www.auxmerveilleux.com

Didier Fourreau page 12
87, rue de Courcelles,
01 47 63 93 05, closed Sunday
www.didierfourreau.com

Gontran Cherrier page 42
8, rue Juliette-Lamber,
01 40 54 72 60, closed Wednesday
www.gontrancherrierboulanger.com

Kaffeehaus page 109
11, rue Poncelet,
01 42 67 07 19, closed Monday
www.kaffeehaus-paris.fr

La Pâtisserie des Rêves pages 31 and 102
19, rue Poncelet,
01 42 67 71 79, closed Monday
www.lapatisseriedesreves.com

Mister Ice page 92
6, rue Descombes, 01 42 67 76 24,
closed Sunday and Monday
www.glacier-foenix.com

Pastelaria Belem page 109
47, rue Boursault,
01 45 22 38 95, closed Monday

18th arrondissement
Arnaud Larher pages 36 and 66
• 53, rue Caulaincourt,
01 42 57 68 08, closed Monday
• 57, rue Damrémont,
01 42 55 57 97, closed Monday
www.arnaud-larher.com

Christophe Roussel page 70
5, rue Tardieu, 01 42 58 91 01
www.christophe-roussel.fr

Gontran Cherrier page 42
22, rue Caulaincourt,
01 46 06 82 66, closed Wednesday
www.gontrancherrierboulanger.com

It Mylk page 88
1, place Suzanne-Valadon, by the lower
funicular station, closed Monday through
Friday
www.itmylk.fr

Maison Landemaine page 49
4, rue du Poteau,
01 42 64 87 78, closed Sunday
www.maisonlandemaine.com

20th arrondissement
La Gambette à Pain page 49
86, avenue Gambetta, 01 43 64 52 34,
closed Saturday and Sunday
'La Gambette À Pain Marque déposée'
on Facebook

La Pâtisserie de l'Église page 16
10, rue du Jourdain, 01 46 36 66 08
www.demoncyvergne.com

L'Atelier des Chefs page 116
Printemps Nation,
21, cours de Vincennes, 01 49 70 97 50
www.atelierdeschefs.fr

77 (Seine-et-Marne)
La Maison du Chocolat pages 36 and 74
La Vallée Village,
3, cours de la Garonne, 77700 Serris
www.lamaisonduchocolat.fr

78 (Yvelines)
Gontran Cherrier page 42
1, rue de la Grande-Fontaine,
78100 Saint-Germain-en-Laye,
01 39 10 89 98, closed Thursday
www.gontrancherrierboulanger.com

Ladurée page 16
• Château de Versailles, 78000 Versailles,
01 30 83 04 02, closed Monday
www.laduree.com

La Maison du Chocolat pages 36 and 74
Parly-2, niveau 1, porte Opéra,
2, avenue Charles-de-Gaulle,
78150 Le Chesnay, closed Sunday
www.lamaisonduchocolat.fr

La Pâtisserie des Rêves pages 31 and 102
Parly-2, 78158 Le Chesnay,
01 39 02 08 63, closed Sunday
www.lapatisseriedesreves.com

Patrick Roger pages 55 and 74
2, rue de Paris, 78100 Saint-Germain-en-
Laye, 01 34 51 72 85, closed Monday
www.patrickroger.com

Pierre Hermé pages 28 and 65
Parly-2, avenue Charles-de-Gaulle,
78150 Le Chesnay, 01 43 54 47 77,
closed Sunday
www.pierreherme.com

91 (Essonne)
La Maison du Chocolat pages 36 and 74
Orly Airport, Terminal Ouest, Hall 2, Gate A,
91550 Orly, 01 49 75 11 10
www.lamaisonduchocolat.fr

Ladurée page 16
• Paris Orly Airport, West Terminal, Hall 2,
91550 Orly, 01 74 22 07 77
www.laduree.com

92 (Hauts-de-Seine)
Patrick Roger pages 55 and 74
47, rue Houdan, 92330 Sceaux,
01 47 02 30 17, closed Monday
www.patrickroger.com

94 (Val-de-Marne)
À la Mère de Famille pages 69 and 92
7, avenue Charles-de-Gaulle,
94100 Saint-Maur, 01 42 83 81 49
www.lameredefamille.com

Baillardran page 23
Orly Airport, Terminal Ouest, Departure
Level, 94310 Orly, 01 49 75 53 04
www.baillardran.com

95 (Val-d'Oise)
It Mylk page 88
Charles-de-Gaulle Airport, Terminal 2E,
Duty-Free Area, Gates L21-L23, 95700
Roissy-en-France
www.itmylk.fr

Ladurée page 16
• Paris Charles-de-Gaulle Airport,
Terminals AC, 2E, 2F, 95700
Roissy-en-France
www.laduree.com

La Maison du Chocolat pages 36 and 74
Charles-de-Gaulle Airport, Terminals
2A-2C, 2E, 2F, 95700 Roissy-en-France
www.lamaisonduchocolat.fr

Le Cacaotier page 65
14, rue de Mora, 95880 Enghien-les-Bains,
01 39 89 29 31, closed Sunday and Monday
www.lecacaotier.com

Angers
Benoît Chocolats page 76
1, rue des Lices, 49100 Angers,
02 41 88 94 52, closed Sunday and Monday
www.chocolats-benoit.com

Bordeaux
Baillardran page 23
• Galerie des Grands-Hommes,
33000 Bordeaux,
05 56 79 05 89, closed Sunday
• Centre commercial Auchan Bordeaux-Lac,
33000 Bordeaux, 05 56 43 29 38
• Centre commercial Mériadeck,
33000 Bordeaux, 05 56 24 68 40
• Gare Bordeaux Saint-Jean,
hall Départ, niveaux 0 et –1,
33000 Bordeaux
• 55, cours de l'Intendance,
33000 Bordeaux, 05 56 52 92 64
• 41, rue des 3-Conils,
33000 Bordeaux, 05 56 44 10 61
• 29, rue Porte-Dijeaux,
33000 Bordeaux, 05 56 52 87 45
• 111, rue Porte-Dijeaux,
33000 Bordeaux, 05 56 51 02 09
www.baillardran.com

Brussels
Patrick Roger pages 55 and 74
Place du Grand-Sablon, 43, 1000 Brussel,
(0032) 2 514 70 46
www.patrickroger.com

Pierre Marcolini page 59
• Avenue de Hinnisdael, 14, 1150 Brussel,
(0032) 2 771 27 20, closed Sunday
• Boulevard de la Woluwe, 28, 1150 Brussel,
(0032) 2 771 20 60
• Chaussée de Waterloo, 1302, 1180
Brussel, (0032) 2 372 15 11,
closed Sunday
• Cour Wiltcher's, avenue Louise, 75 M,
1050 Brussel, (0032) 2 538 42 24,
closed Sunday
• Gare Eurostar, rue de France, 2,
1060 Brussel, (0032) 2 523 58 97
• Galerie de la Reine, 21,
1000 Brussel, (0032) 2 502 35 67

• Place du Grand-Sablon, 39,
1000 Brussel, (0032) 2 513 17 83,
closed Monday
• Rue des Minimes, 1, place du Grand-
Sablon, 1000 Brussel, (0032) 2 514 12 06
www.marcolini.com

Deauville
Martine Lambert page 95
76 bis, rue Eugène-Colas,
14800 Deauville, 02 31 88 94 04
www.martine-lambert.com

Dijon
Fabrice Gillotte page 73
21, rue du Bourg, 21000 Dijon,
03 80 30 38 88, closed Sunday
www.fabrice-gillotte.fr

La Baule
Christophe Roussel page 70
• 6, allée des Camélias,
44500 La Baule, 02 40 60 65 04
• 19, avenue Charles-de-Gaulle,
44500 La Baule, 02 40 23 10 84
www.christophe-roussel.fr

Le Comptoir Baulois page 23
131, avenue du Général-de-Gaulle,
44500 La Baule-Escoublac,
02 40 23 16 05, closed Monday
www.lefondantbaulois.com

Lille
Aux Merveilleux de Fred page 20
• Café Méo, 5-7, Grand'Place, 59000 Lille,
06 73 88 60 10, closed Monday
• 67, rue de la Monnaie, 59000 Lille,
03 20 51 99 59, closed Monday
• 336, rue Léon-Gambetta, 59000 Lille,
03 20 57 25 58
www.auxmerveilleux.com

Meert page 20
27, rue Esquermoise, 59000 Lille,
03 20 57 07 44, closed Monday
www.meert.fr

Quiberon
Henri Le Roux pages 70 and 84
18, rue de Port-Maria, 56170 Quiberon,
02 97 50 06 83, closed Sunday and Monday
www.chocolatleroux.com

Roanne
Maison Pralus pages 46 and 56
• Les Halles Diderot, 42300 Roanne,
04 77 67 69 02, closed Monday
• 8, rue Charles-de-Gaulle,
42300 Roanne, 04 77 71 24 10,
closed Sunday and Monday
www.chocolats-pralus.com

Saint-Jean-de-Luz
Pariès pages 23 and 83
9, rue Gambetta, 64500 Saint-Jean-de-Luz,
05 59 26 01 46
www.paries.fr

Sarreguemines
Franck Kestener page 59
6, rue Gutenberg, 57200 Sarreguemines,
03 87 28 14 62,
closed Sunday and Monday
www.franck-kestener.com

LES GUIDES DU CHÊNE

DES GUIDES PAS COMME LES AUTRES

EXISTE EN VERSION **NUMÉRIQUE**

My little Paris
My Little Paris, Kanako
Les meilleures adresses secrètes
et insolites des Parisiennes !

My little Paris
My Little Paris, Kanako
The Paris only Parisians know!

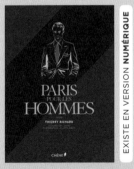

EXISTE EN VERSION **NUMÉRIQUE**

Paris pour les hommes
Thierry Richard, Aseyn,
Juliette Ranck
Le premier city guide conçu
pour vous, les hommes...
qui aimez Paris et ses plaisirs.

Paris for men
Thierry Richard, Aseyn,
Juliette Ranck
The first city guide for men
who love Paris.

EXISTE EN VERSION **NUMÉRIQUE**

Paris à Vélib'

7 itinéraires cyclables
pour découvrir Paris
autrement.

Paris by bike

Seven cycle routes for
exploring Paris.

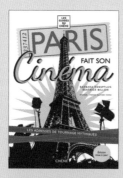

Paris fait son cinéma

Barbara Boespflug, Beatrice Billon,
Pierre-Olivier Signe

Le guide des 101 adresses
mythiques qui ont inspiré
les plus grands films.

The film lover's Paris

Barbara Boespflug, Beatrice Billon,
Pierre-Olivier Signe

101 legendary adresses that
inspired great movies.

New York fait son cinéma

Barbara Boespflug, Beatrice Billon,
Pierre Olivier Signe

60 adresses mythiques qui
ont inspiré les plus grands
films à New York.

The film lover's New York

Barbara Boespflug, Beatrice Billon,
Pierre Olivier Signe

60 legendary addresses that
inspired great movies.

Original edition published in 2014 by Éditions du Chêne
© Éditions du Chêne – Hachette Livre, 2014
www.editionsduchene.fr

Managing Editor: Valérie Tognali
Assistant Editor: Françoise Mathay
Translation from French: Lyn Thompson Lemaire and Robyn Cahill
Proofreading: Rebecca Brite
Art Direction : Sabine Houplain assisted by Claire Mieyeville
Design and Layout: Gaëlle Junius
Photoengraving: APS Chromostyle
Production: Marion Lance
Partnerships and Direct Sales: Mathilde Barrois (mbarrois@hachette-livre.fr)
Press Relations: Hélène Maurice (hmaurice@hachette-livre.fr)

Published by Éditions du Chêne
(43 quai de Grenelle, 75905 Paris Cedex 15)
Printed in June 2014 by Estella Graficas in Spain
Copyright Registration: August 2014
ISBN 978-2-81231-144-4
56/0004/3-01